D0336243

Functional Skills

Information Communication Technology

(ICT) Level 2

Step-By-Step Guide

in

Office 2010 & Windows 7

By
Lorna Bointon

Qualiteach Education

2014

THE MANCHESTER COLLEGE
COLLEGE LIBRARIES
ASHTON OLD ROAD
MANCHESTER
M11 2WH

© Lorna Bointon, Qualiteach Education 2014

ISBN: 978-0-9565731-4-8

A catalogue record for this book is available from the British Library

RECEIVED
30 JUN 2014
14:99

Published by
Qualiteach Education
Tel. 0800 612 5438
E-mail: contact@qualiteach.co.uk
Web: www.qualiteach.co.uk

First Published   2014

All rights reserved. No part of this publication may be reproduced, stored in a retrieval system or transmitted, in any form or by any means without the prior written permission of the publisher, nor be otherwise circulated in any form of binding or cover other than that in which it is published and without a similar being imposed on any subsequent purchase or user.

Microsoft ® Windows®, Microsoft® Office, Microsoft® Office Word 2010, Microsoft® Office Access 2010, Microsoft® Office Excel 2010, Microsoft® Office PowerPoint 2010, Microsoft® Office Outlook 2010 and Microsoft® Internet Explorer are either registered trademarks or trademarks of the Microsoft corporation. Windows® is a registered trademark of Microsoft Corporation in the United States and other countries

Functional Skills ICT Level 2 is an independent publication and is not affiliated with, nor has it been authorized, sponsored, or otherwise approved by the Microsoft Corporation.

The companies, organisations, products, the related people, their positions, names, addresses and details used for instructional purposes in the manual and its related support materials on the Web are fictitious. No association with any real company, organisations, products or people are intended nor should be inferred.

Credits

Author
Lorna Bointon

Editor
Richard Bointon

IMPORTANT

No part of this publication may be photocopied or reproduced in any form without the prior written permission of the publisher, in accordance with copyright law.

ABOUT THIS BOOK

The Level 2 Functional Skills Step-By-Step Guide is intended as a progression from Level 1 with some prior knowledge assumed. Therefore, although there is some crossover between the two levels, students should refer to the Level 1 Step-By-Step Guide where basic instruction and background knowledge is required. Other Functional Skills resources at Level 1 and Level 2 are available from Qualiteach Education. Schools and colleges may purchase a site licence allowing unlimited photocopying of training materials, such as build-up exercises, practice papers and reference guides.

Contents

vi

Section 1 ▶

Using ICT

Plan

Plan solutions to complex tasks by analysing the necessary stages

Use ICT to Plan and Analyse Tasks

Did You Know?

Effective planning ensures a successful result

Why is planning important?

ICT can be used to plan and analyse complex or multi-step tasks and activities. It is important to plan a task thoroughly beforehand to ensure the following:

- there is enough time to complete the task
- there are enough resources at your disposal to complete the task. Resources can be:
  - People
  - Money
  - Equipment
  - Time
- issues are recognised and accounted for, such as security issues or urgent time frames/deadlines
- contingency plans are put in place to deal with unforeseen issues (higher costs, deadlines not met, supply problems)
- training is arranged and provided to meet the needs of the users

What type of tasks may need planning?

Tasks that need planning range from straightforward tasks, such as making a purchase, to more complex tasks, such as planning a computer network or a website.

See the examples below of some complex and multi-step tasks:

- **Websites** – need to be planned thoroughly beforehand to ensure effective navigation
- **Computer network** –needs careful planning at each step to ensure that all aspects are covered, such as timescales, costs and training.
- **Trips**– need to be planned in detail to ensure that they run smoothly (e.g. date, destination, time, cost, transport)
- **Charity events** –need meticulous planning to ensure that advertising attracts maximum interest and attendance. Thorough planning and research is required for this task to ensure that health and safety regulations and insurance requirements are met. Volunteers need to be arranged and organised
- **File structure** – planning how you will store files and folders ensures an organised filing system

ICT planning tools
- Word processor: create a timetable, storyboard or a mind map
- Spreadsheet: work out costs and timescales or create a Gantt chart
- PowerPoint presentation: create hierarchical charts to show the priority of each part of the task

   © Lorna Bointon, Qualiteach Education 2014

Scheduling

Creating a schedule is an important part of the planning process and helps to ensure that enough time is allocated to enable successful completion of the task. Scheduling tools include project management tools, timetables and Gantt charts.

Timetable

A timetable displays the task name, the estimated day and time that the task will be completed and a column which can be ticked to indicate that the task is complete. See the example below of a timetable:

> *Ahmed is organising a trip for a group of friends to a place of interest, which will include transport to and from the destination and booking lunch at a local cafe.*

Task	Day	Source	Time	Task complete ✓	Notes
Arrange date and destination of trip	Mon	Text, email or speak directly	7pm	☐	Meet mates at Ben's place or text
Finalise destination and visit to place of interest	Tues	Internet	9-10	☐	Look up proposed destination and places of interest to visit
Find entry costs and opening times	Tues	Internet	10-11	☐	Work out times/costs for entry to place of interest
Find transport costs and book transport	Tues	Internet/Yellow Pages	11-12	☐	Ring or email for transport costs
Book lunch	Tues	Internet	12-1	☐	Email or ring local cafes for menu details and prices and book online if necessary
Email friends to confirm	Wed	Email or text	9-10	☐	Send email or text to confirm trip

Gantt chart

A Gantt chart is a stacked horizontal bar chart, created using spreadsheet software, which shows the schedule of a small project, such as the task, the duration of the task and the hierarchy (order of priority or importance). The current status of a task is displayed along with start/end dates or times for the project. This helps the user to see the project's ongoing progression and development.

 © Lorna Bointon, Qualiteach Education 2014

The Gantt chart below is based on the following schedule for the day trip:

TASK	START	DURATION	
Arrive Depot	9:00	0.15	9:00am to 9:15am
Journey	9:15	2	9:15 am to 11:15am
Lunch	12:00	1	12am to 1:00 pm
Games Exhibition	13:30	1.5	1:30pm to 3:00pm
Travel Home	15:30	2	3:30pm to 5:30pm

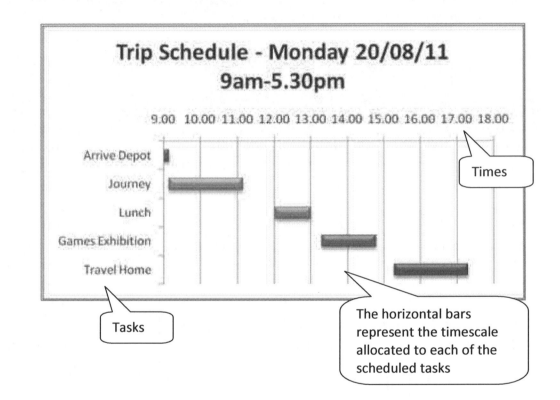

Storyboard

A storyboard is a rough design or initial plan of a movie, project, newsletter or other media that requires a design, such as a website. In the example below, a storyboard is created for a website:

HOME PAGE:

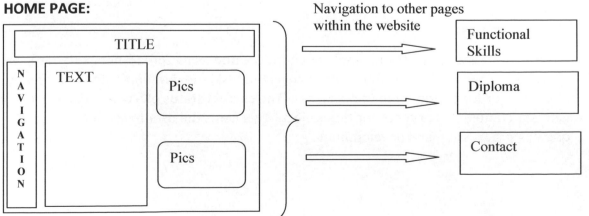

Completed home page:

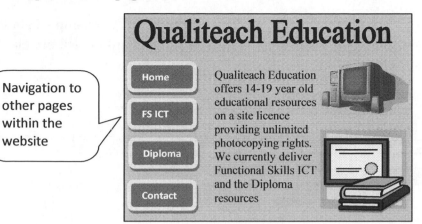

Navigation to other pages within the website

Mind Map

A mind map is a visual way of showing the thought processes involved in planning a project (sometimes referred to as 'brainstorming') and helps to break down each part of a task in the form of routes radiating from the central idea/concept. This method is supposed to aid creative thought. See the example below (thought processes to aid planning/development of a computer network):

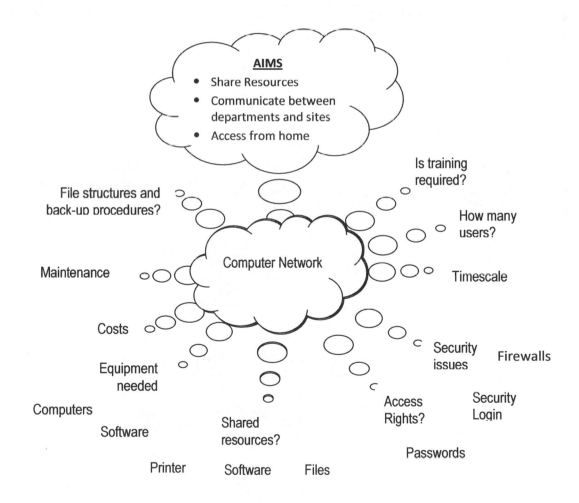

© Lorna Bointon, Qualiteach Education 2014

Spreadsheet

A spreadsheet is a great tool to help you work out costs of a task. In the example below the projected profits from a forthcoming Teddy Bear Parachute Jump charity event are planned and analysed in a spreadsheet:

	A	B	C	D
1	**Teddy Bear Parachute Jump**			
2				
3	**August Bank Holiday 2010**			
4				
5	**Price Per Jump**	£1.00		
6				
7				
8	**EXPENDITURE**			
9	Insurance	£150.00		
10	Stall	£20.00		
11	Stationery	£100.00		
12	Advertising	£100.00		
13	TOTAL	£370.00		
14				
15				
16	**INCOME**			
17	Amount of jumps	1050		
18	TOTAL	£1,050.00		
19				
20	**PROFIT**	£680.00		
21				

Hierarchical chart

A hierarchical chart is one that shows tasks or an organisation's workforce in order of importance or priority. A hierarchical or organisation chart may also be used to indicate the hierarchy within an organisation, for example:

 © Lorna Bointon, Qualiteach Education 2014

Flowcharts and diagrams may also be used to plan a file management structure on your computer. For example, Qualiteach Education stores files received electronically from suppliers, such as delivery notes and invoices, and files which the company sends out to customers, such as letters and invoices. These files need to be stored in an organised manner in order to access them easily and quickly. The files are listed below:

- Letters to customers
- Invoices to customers
- Delivery notes from suppliers
- Invoices from suppliers.

The flowchart/diagram below displays a sample file structure for the storage of files listed above:

FILE STRUCTURE

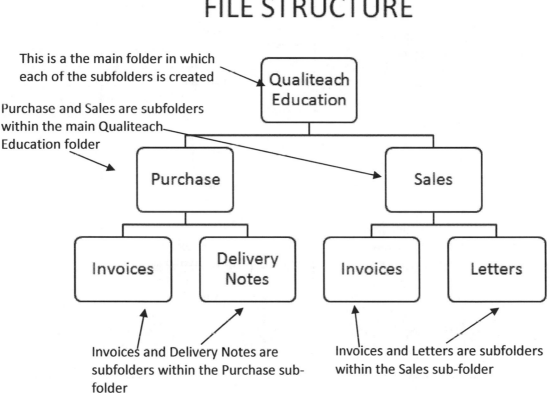

This is a the main folder in which each of the subfolders is created

Purchase and Sales are subfolders within the main Qualiteach Education folder

Invoices and Delivery Notes are subfolders within the Purchase sub-folder

Invoices and Letters are subfolders within the Sales sub-folder

Summary

The following summary uses the creation of a computer network within a small company as an example.

Plan a computer network:

A *mind map* can be used initially to visualise the idea/concept and break down each part of a task. This helps to generate ideas and encourages positive interaction and involvement with other users. Some of the ideas that may be explored using a mind map are:

- Why is it needed?
- Would another solution work better?

Taking ideas down different routes may result in a different outcome to the one expected.

© Lorna Bointon, Qualiteach Education 2014

- Local or Wide Area Network?
- Security Issues – passwords, access rights, access to external users, backing up data
- What information should be stored and what should be shared? This may include software, printers, communication and files
- What equipment is needed? Computers, printers, server, software – this is linked to costs (see below)
- File structures – how should files be stored?
- Timescale –work out the best time to start and finish the project. Will it disrupt workflow?
- Costs – work out expenditure and staff costs
- Training – will users need to be trained? This should be included in the timescale and costs.
- Who will maintain the network system?

A rough design or **storyboard** can be created to display how the network will be created:

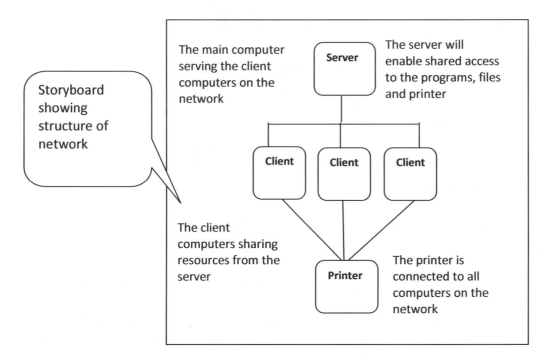

A **timetable** or **Gantt chart** can be used to detail the timescale involved and the order of priority or importance of each task in the schedule.

A **flowchart** can be used which shows each person's responsibilities for specific tasks (maintenance etc).

A **spreadsheet** can be used to work out costs.

A **diagram** can be used to display file/folder structure.

Checklist:

- ICT to plan timescales – Gantt chart, timetables
- ICT to plan layout or structure – storyboard, diagram, flowchart
- ICT to plan costs – spreadsheets
- ICT to arrange ideas/concepts – mind map

© Lorna Bointon, Qualiteach Education 2014

Have a Go

Try the activities below to test yourself on the previous section

Match Makers

Match the correct planning method with the description below:

1.	Planning a layout or structure	a.	Gantt Chart
2.	Planning costs	b.	Storyboard
3.	Planning a schedule	c.	Mind Map
4.	Visualising ideas	d.	Spreadsheet

Add your answers below (e.g. 1a etc):

1.		2.		3.		4.	

You are planning a trip for yourself and friends. Arrange the planning tasks below into order of priority:

a	b	c	d	e
Book transport	Book Lunch	Confirm amount of people on trip	Work out time schedule	Arrange a date

1.

2.

3.

4.

5.

 © Lorna Bointon, Qualiteach Education 2014

As Easy As....

1. A Gantt chart is a planning tool for which of the following?

A	A schedule for a project	☐
B	Brainstorming ideas	☐
C	A rough design or storyboard	☐
D	Working out costs	☐

2a. Which of the following ICT tools would you use in the planning stage of website creation?

A	Storyboard	☐
B	Mind map	☐
C	Timetable	☐
D	Hierarchy Chart	☐

2b. State the reasons for your choice

3. Which of the following statements is appropriate to planning a task?

A	Work out purpose and objectives	☐
B	Recognise intended audience	☐
C	Ensure accessibility and security	☐
D	All of the above	☐

4. When planning a website, what is the most important aspect?

A	Navigation structure	☐
B	Multiple pages	☐
C	Pictures	☐
D	Large fonts	☐

 © Lorna Bointon, Qualiteach Education 2014

Section 2 ▶
Using ICT

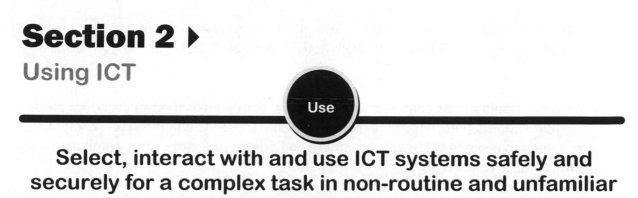

Use

Select, interact with and use ICT systems safely and securely for a complex task in non-routine and unfamiliar contexts

Use Software Applications

Did You Know?

Many new applications are available free for a trial period

> **NOTE:** For details of individual software applications and examples of output, see the **Level 1** Functional Skills Activity Workbook and Revision Guide

Software should not be confused with hardware. Hardware is the term used for physical computer components which the user can touch. These include the actual computer and computer screen and the keyboard, mouse and printer (the latter three components are referred to as *peripherals*).

Software applications are computer programs designed to perform tasks and solve complex problems. Software programs need to be installed onto a computer, usually in the Program Files folder on the hard drive. Most software programs will run automatically when the CD/DVD is inserted and a series of windows will appear on screen to guide the user through the installation and setup procedure. A software program is stored using RAM (Random-Access Memory; also referred to as *volatile memory*) a temporary memory store which loses data when the computer is switched off. The CPU loads each program into RAM before running each line of the program consecutively. This means that more temporary memory is required for each software program that is run, which can result in slower performance. To ensure that your computer runs quickly and smoothly when handling multiple software programs, you should ensure that there is enough RAM (memory upgrades can be purchased and installed easily).

These are **hardware** components

Software programs are stored on the hard drive of the computer.

Operating System Software

A computer needs to have operating system software before application software, such as Microsoft Word, can be installed. The operating system manages computer programs and provides an interface to enable interaction between the computer and the user. The most common interface is a GUI or Graphical User Interface used by Microsoft Windows (e.g. the desktop displays icons, menus and toolbars). The operating system also manages input and output from peripheral devices such as keyboard, mouse etc. The operating system is initially loaded by a 'boot' program called BIOS. Examples of operating systems are shown below:

- Microsoft Windows XP, Vista, Microsoft Windows 7
- Linux (open source software)
- Apple Mac OS

Application Software

There are many types of software applications available for different purposes. Software applications are also referred to as *programs*.

Software applications are computer programs designed to perform a particular task. For example:

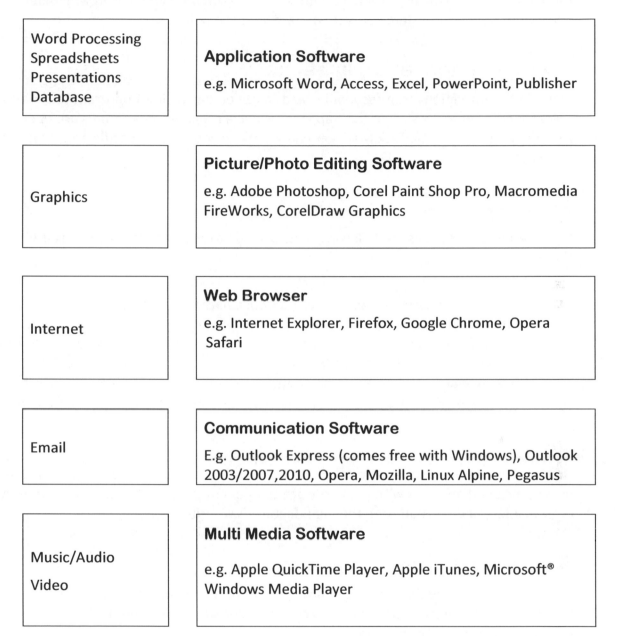

Word Processing Spreadsheets Presentations Database	**Application Software** e.g. Microsoft Word, Access, Excel, PowerPoint, Publisher
Graphics	**Picture/Photo Editing Software** e.g. Adobe Photoshop, Corel Paint Shop Pro, Macromedia FireWorks, CorelDraw Graphics
Internet	**Web Browser** e.g. Internet Explorer, Firefox, Google Chrome, Opera Safari
Email	**Communication Software** E.g. Outlook Express (comes free with Windows), Outlook 2003/2007,2010, Opera, Mozilla, Linux Alpine, Pegasus
Music/Audio Video	**Multi Media Software** e.g. Apple QuickTime Player, Apple iTunes, Microsoft® Windows Media Player

 © Lorna Bointon, Qualiteach Education 2014

Software Versions

There are different versions of software being created all the time. For example, Microsoft Office 97, Microsoft Office 2003, Microsoft Office 2007 and Microsoft Office 2010 are versions of the same software which has been updated over the years to keep up with technological progress. Software updates include greater functionality and capability but there may be compatibility problems with some new software when used with older versions of operating system software or hardware components.

Managing Active Applications

Sometimes applications stop responding and freeze or 'hang'. It is important to shut down un-responding programs when this happens. When a program or programs are open it is referred to as *active*. The Task Manager enables the user to select specific programs and close them.

Security Software

Security software such as the following is installed on a computer to prevent security threats:

- **Firewall** – blocks unauthorised access from a hacker
- **Anti-virus software** – prevents viruses from downloading onto your computer. Anti-virus software will identify and then disinfect a virus threat. Examples are Norton Anti-Virus, AVG and McAfee Virus Scan
- **Anti-spyware** – to prevent tracking and monitoring of a user via online activity or keystrokes. Examples of anti-spyware programs are Windows Defender and AVG

Drivers

Drivers are programs that enable computer hardware to function correctly. Drivers are usually included on a disk with the hardware component, such as digital camera or printer, or available as a download from the manufacturer's website.

Shareware/Freeware

Shareware is software that a user can download onto their computer for a trial period before purchasing a software licence. Freeware is software that is totally free to use and does not require a software licence.

Keeping it legal

When software is legally installed on a computer, it is allocated a Product ID number to show that it is registered. An **End User Agreement** provides legal details regarding permission of use. A single software licence gives a user the right to install and use the software on their computer. A multi-user site licence allows the software to be installed and used by a specified number of users on a computer network. A licence holder does not have the right to share the software with anyone else. Unauthorised copying and sharing of software is referred to as **software piracy**.

 © Lorna Bointon, Qualiteach Education 2014

Checklist:

- ✓ Operating System software includes Microsoft Windows and Linux
- ✓ Application software includes word processing, spreadsheets, databases, presentations
- ✓ Communications software includes e-mail
- ✓ Software that enables a user to browse the Internet is called a web browser
- ✓ Graphics software is used to edit and format pictures and photographs
- ✓ Multi-media software enables a user to download video and audio files
- ✓ Security software prevents security threats on your computer
- ✓ Anti-virus software prevents malicious threats and viruses from damaging your computer

 © Lorna Bointon, Qualiteach Education 2014

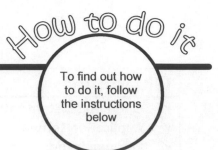

Open an application

1.   To open an application, select the **Start** menu

2.   Select **All Programs** ▶ and then the folder in which the program/application is stored (e.g. the **Microsoft Office** folder or the **iTunes** folder)

3.   Select the application from the sub-menu

The application may be saved on the desktop as an icon – if this is the case, just double click the application icon to launch the program.

Install/uninstall application software

1.   To un-install an application, select the **Start** menu

2.   Select **Control Panel** and then select **Programs.**

3.   Under **Programs and Features,** select **Uninstall Programs.** Select the application that you want to un-install and click **Uninstall.** Confirm that you want to uninstall the selected program.

4.   To install a new program, insert the CD or DVD containing the program into the correct drive and then follow the on-screen instructions for setup and installation. Most programs on a CD/DVD have an AutoPlay facility which starts an installation Wizard.

Manage un-responding applications

1.   Right click an empty area of the Task Bar and select **Start Task Manager**

2.   Select a program and then click **End Task**.

3.   Confirm that you want to end the program now.

2.1 Activities

Match Makers

Match the questions below to the correct answer:

1.	Shareware	a.	Firewall to prevent unauthorised access to a computer system
2.	Application software	b.	Software that manages files and programs on a computer
3.	Security software	c.	A program designed to perform a task such as create documents, spreadsheets and databases
4.	Freeware	d.	Software enabling communication with other users using email and Internet
5.	Multi-media software	e.	Software that can be used for a trial period before purchase
6.	Operating system software	f.	Software enabling a user to play and view videos and audio files
7.	Communication software	g.	Software that is free to use without a software licence

Add your answers below (e.g. 1a etc):

1.	
2.	
3.	
4.	
5.	
6.	
7.	

As Easy As....

1. Software programs are stored in which type of temporary memory store which loses data when the computer is switched off?

A	ROM	☐
B	EPROM	☐
C	RAM	☐
D	E-RAM	☐

2. This software manages input and output from peripheral devices?

A	Application	☐
B	Multi-media	☐
C	Operating System	☐
D	Communication	☐

3. Unauthorised copying of software is known by which name?

A	Software Thieving	☐
B	Software Piracy	☐
C	Software Robbing	☐
D	Software Smuggling	☐

4. What is the name of the device used to manage un-responsive applications?

A	Performance Manager	☐
B	Task Manager	☐
C	Work Manager	☐
D	File Manager	☐

 © Lorna Bointon, Qualiteach Education 2014

Select and Use Interface Features & System Facilities

Did You Know?

GUI stands for Graphical User Interface

An interface is the front end of a program which allows a user to interact with an ICT device such as:

- the desktop in Microsoft Windows® 7
- the screen on a mobile phone or other mobile device

> Mobile devices include laptops and notebook computers, along with handheld devices such as the following:
> - Palm tops
> - PDAs (Personal Digital Assistant)
> - Mobile phones – full browser capability is available on some mobile phones
>
> A handheld device has a display screen with keyboard or touch screen interface. Mobile devices can connect to the Internet wherever there is a WI-FI hotspot, such as a shopping centre, hotel, airport etc.

- an ATM machine (Automatic Teller Machine or cash dispenser)
    - An ATM (or Automatic Teller Machine) is a machine, widely available outside banks, supermarkets and many other locations, that enables customers to withdraw cash, using a debit or credit card, or view an account balance even when the bank is closed.

Users interact with an ATM using an interface - the user touches on-screen options and a result is displayed on-screen.

Another example of an interface is a touch screen used in an EPOS system (Electronic Point of Sale) which is used in self check-outs in supermarkets. The user touches options on the screen to control the output (enter price, enter amount of cash received, the machine will calculate amount of change to be returned). The printed output is a receipt of the transaction.

Microsoft Windows

The Microsoft Windows desktop displays a GUI Interface (Graphical User Interface) which is a user-friendly display enabling a user to interact by clicking icons or opening menus.

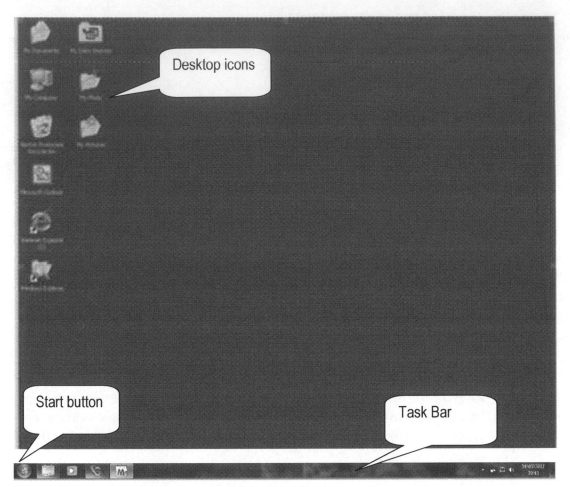

The Windows interface displays the following:

- Icons
- Windows
- Menus
- Dialog boxes
- Buttons
- Tool Bars/Ribbon
- Scroll Bars
- Zoom Bar
- Keypads
- Touch screens

Tip:

An icon represents a program, file, printer, drive or folder. To open a file, folder or program, double click the icon or right click and select **Open**.

> **NOTE:** See the **Level 1** Functional Skills Activity Workbook and Revision Guide for examples of Windows Interface features, such as icons and dialog boxes

 © Lorna Bointon, Qualiteach Education 2014

Changing the Microsoft Windows Desktop Interface

The colour, style or size of interface features, such as background, icons or menus, can be altered to suit the user.

Select **Start** and then **Control** Panel and choose **Appearance and Personalization.**
Alternatively, right click the desktop and choose **Personalize** to do any of the following:

- Resize icons and other Windows items
- Change style of icons, menus, windows
- Change background

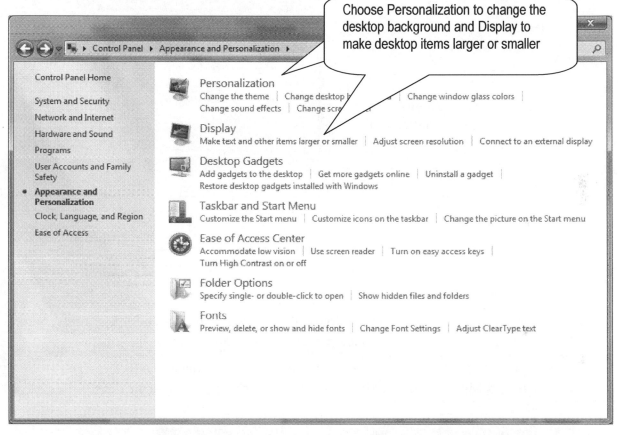

Choose Personalization to change the desktop background and Display to make desktop items larger or smaller

Icon size can be increased or decreased by right clicking the desktop, selecting **View** and then choosing **Small, Medium** or **Large.**

Icons can be moved to another position on the desktop by dragging the icon into position. The Auto Arrange feature which keeps the icons in place needs to be turned off first. To check that **Auto Arrange** is *off* right click the desktop and choose **View** and then see if there is a tick beside the **Auto Arrange Icons** menu option. A tick means that Auto Arrange Icons is *on.* Click the Auto Arrange Icon menu option to turn it *off.*

 © Lorna Bointon, Qualiteach Education 2014

The Help Facility

Microsoft Windows Help facility displays helpful information and guidance on topics entered by a user, either within an application such as Microsoft Word or through the Help Centre in My Computer. Demonstrations and tutorials are also available.

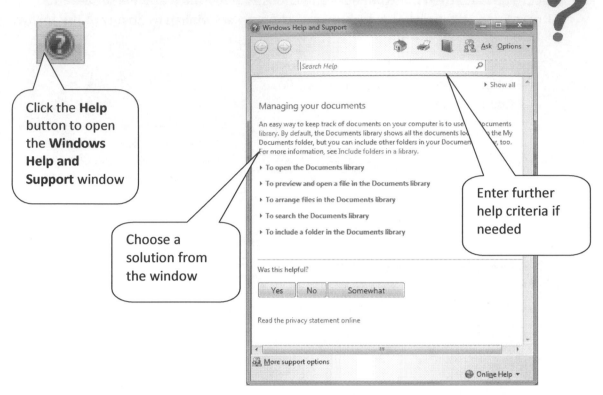

Click the **Help** button to open the **Windows Help and Support** window

Choose a solution from the window

Enter further help criteria if needed

Search Facility

The Search facility in Microsoft Windows allows the user to search for files and folders using partial file names, file types, file sizes, date saved or file location.

This feature is very handy when you can't find a file and only know that it starts with a 'p', is a Microsoft Word document and was saved on a specific date.

1) Choose a location in which to search

2) Enter the file name here and, as you type, a list of files containing the typed characters is listed below (e.g. if you type **data**, all files containing these characters will be listed

database2

Add a search filter

Authors: Type: Date modified: Size:

3) As you type, the **Add a search filter** menu opens. Click a search filter to search by author, date modified, file type or file size.

Match Makers

Match the correct description with the Windows item below:

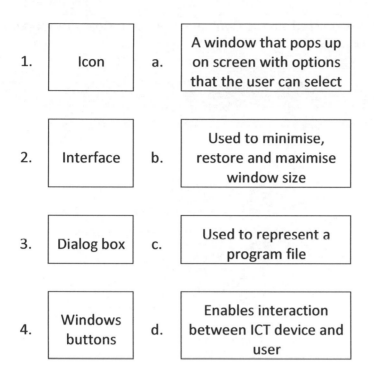

1. Icon — a. A window that pops up on screen with options that the user can select

2. Interface — b. Used to minimise, restore and maximise window size

3. Dialog box — c. Used to represent a program file

4. Windows buttons — d. Enables interaction between ICT device and user

Enter your answers below:

1.		2.		3.		4.	

As Easy As....

A B C

1. The Microsoft Windows desktop is an example of?

A	A Graphical User Interface	☐
B	A DOS program	☐
C	Application software.	☐
D	Multi-media software	☐

Adjust System Settings

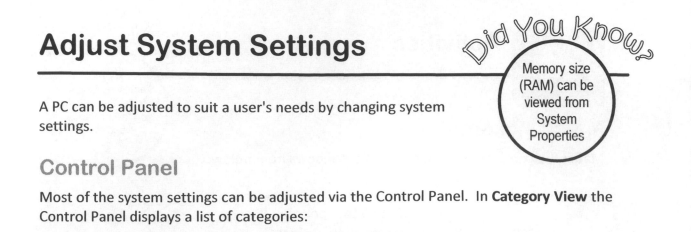

Did You Know?

Memory size (RAM) can be viewed from System Properties

A PC can be adjusted to suit a user's needs by changing system settings.

Control Panel

Most of the system settings can be adjusted via the Control Panel. In **Category View** the Control Panel displays a list of categories:

System and Security

Schedule regular maintenance checks, increase space on your hard disk, or configure energy-saving settings.

- Firewall settings and status
- Troubleshoot computer problems
- Windows updates and schedule tasks
- Back-up and Restore
- Administrative Tools (free up disk space etc)

Automatic Updates: can be set to be installed at specific times

Network and Internet Connections

Connect to the Internet, create a home or small office network, configure network settings to work from home, or change modem, phone or Internet settings.

- Internet Options
- Network Connections
- Sharing Options

Hardware and Sound

Add or remove printers or other hardware devices. Change the entire sound scheme or individual sounds made by your computer, or configure the settings for your speakers and recording devices.

- Devices and Printers
- Mouse
- AutoPlay (for installing programs from CD/DVD)
- Sounds and Audio Devices
- Power Options
- Display (screen resolution etc)

Volume: can be increased, decreased or muted as required

Programs

Uninstall computer programs or components

Mouse settings: can be adjusted to make it easier to see the mouse arrow; for example, make the mouse speed slower and apply a 'tail' so that the arrow can be seen clearly

User Accounts and Family Safety

Change user account settings, passwords and pictures.

- Mail
- Set up parental controls
- User Accounts

 © Lorna Bointon, Qualiteach Education 2014

Appearance and Personalization

Change the appearance of desktop items, apply a theme or screen saver for your computer, or customise the Start menu and taskbar. Within this category you can change the following settings:

- Display
- Taskbar and Start Menu
- Folder options
- Fonts
- Monitor display

Colour themes: can be changed, so that the desktop, windows and other features are displayed in a different colour or formatted to display a picture (desktop)

Picture quality/screen resolution: important when playing multi-media or games software to maximise picture quality

Desktop contrast: can be adjusted to help users with visual impairment

Icon size: can be increased to help users with visual impairment

Clock, Language and Region

Change the date, time, and time zone for your computer, the language to use, and the way numbers, currencies, dates and times are displayed.

- Date & Time
- Region and Language

Clock: can be adjusted to display a different time or time zone

Calendar: can be adjusted to display a different date or date format

Keyboard settings: can be set to required language

Ease of Access

Adjust your computer settings for vision, hearing and mobility.

- Accessibility Options
  - Optimize visual display
  - Change mouse and keyboard settings
  - Use speech recognition and set up a microphone

 © Lorna Bointon, Qualiteach Education 2014

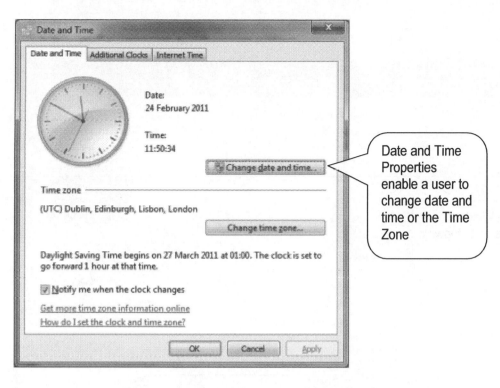

Date and Time Properties enable a user to change date and time or the Time Zone

System Properties

The Control Panel displays the system information for your computer, such as the operating system software, the product ID and computer information such as the processor speed and the amount of RAM (temporary memory) currently installed. To see system properties, do the following:

- Open the Control Panel
- Select **System and Security**
- Select **System** to see the computer manufacturer and other details (such as model and processor speed), the operating system version, the amount of RAM (memory) and the Product ID

   © Lorna Bointon, Qualiteach Education 2014

The Windows version is shown here

System Properties displays information about your computer, such as Manufacturer, Model, Processor type, Installed memory (RAM) and system type

 © Lorna Bointon, Qualiteach Education 2014

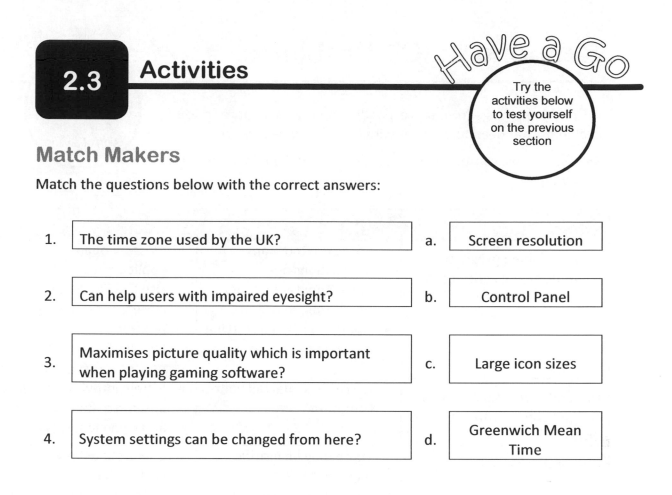

Match Makers

Match the questions below with the correct answers:

1.	The time zone used by the UK?	a.	Screen resolution
2.	Can help users with impaired eyesight?	b.	Control Panel
3.	Maximises picture quality which is important when playing gaming software?	c.	Large icon sizes
4.	System settings can be changed from here?	d.	Greenwich Mean Time

Enter your answers below (e.g. 1a etc):

1.	
2.	
3.	
4.	

As Easy As....

1. Automatic Updates can be set in which window?

A	My Computer	☐
B	Windows Explorer	☐
C	Desktop Properties	☐
D	Control Panel	☐

 © Lorna Bointon, Qualiteach Education 2014

Respond to ICT Problems

Did You Know?

Unfamiliar messages appearing may be the sign of a virus

ICT problems range from un-responding programs to more serious problems that need to be dealt with by a skilled technician.

The symptoms, causes and solutions of ICT problems include the following:

Symptom	Possible Cause	Solution
Un-responding programs, computer hangs or freezes	• There are too many applications open. • The computer memory needs upgrading. • Another program is trying to run in the background.	• Close all open applications. • Use the Task Manager to close un-responding programs. • Install more memory to boost performance
Unfamiliar messages appear, computer performance slows down	• A virus has infected your computer	• Install anti-virus software and run a scan to detect and remove threats
Printer displays a flashing light Printer does not power up or print Prints blank pages, displays streaks or text is not visible	• There may be insufficient paper in the tray • There may be a paper jam • Drivers may need to be installed • Printer cable may not be attached securely in the port • The document may contain blank pages • A new cartridge may be required	• Check paper tray and replenish if necessary. Check that printer is ON! • Before checking for a paper jam, turn off printer and ensure that it has cooled down. Tease paper from rollers **very** carefully. Ask for help from a skilled technician. • Replace the cartridge. • Check that the cable is securely attached to the computer and the printer. • Check document for blank pages and delete. • Install driver software from disk or from manufacturer's website.
Keyboard beeps	• A stuck key or keyboard needs cleaning	• Turn keyboard upside down and shake to remove loose debris. Use a small soft brush to clean between keys. Connect the keyboard to another computer to see if problem is with keyboard or the computer.

Checking

Check for the following:

- Is computer on? Check for a green light on the monitor. Check power supply
- Is the mouse cursor working? Clean the ball in a roller-ball mouse and check that cable is connected properly or check the batteries in an optical or wireless mouse
- Are all cables secured in correct ports? Check all cables
- Is a blank screen due to a screen saver? Wiggle the mouse or press the Spacebar
- Do messages appear on screen? Make a note of messages and error codes
- Check that printer is on, contains enough paper and that the cartridge has sufficient toner
- Has new hardware been installed? Check that correct driver software is installed
- Check for updates to your software on the supplier's website (called patches)

Reporting

It is important to be aware of which problems can be dealt with by an inexperienced user – for example, by using the Task Manager to shut down an un-responding program – and which problems should be reported. If the problem occurs in work or at college, it should be reported to the ICT manager or technician who is responsible for maintaining the computer system. Your place of work or training centre should have a reporting procedure in place and provide a reporting form that can be filled in with details of the problem. If the problem occurs at home with your own personal computer, contact the help desk number provided by the manufacturer or by the store. You could also look on the manufacturer's website to see if they have any advice in their FAQ or troubleshooting sections. The manufacturer's guidelines (which should be provided when you buy a computer or other ICT device) should give some advice on maintenance and use of the device.

When reporting an ICT problem, ensure that the following details are provided:

REPORTING ICT PROBLEMS

You should supply the following:

- Make and model of computer, type and version of software installed
- Date and time that problem occurred
- Location (room number and/or computer name/number if problem occurs in work or college)
- Description of problem
- Steps you have taken to resolve it
- Error messages or codes.

 © Lorna Bointon, Qualiteach Education 2014

Match Makers

Match the symptoms below to the correct solution:

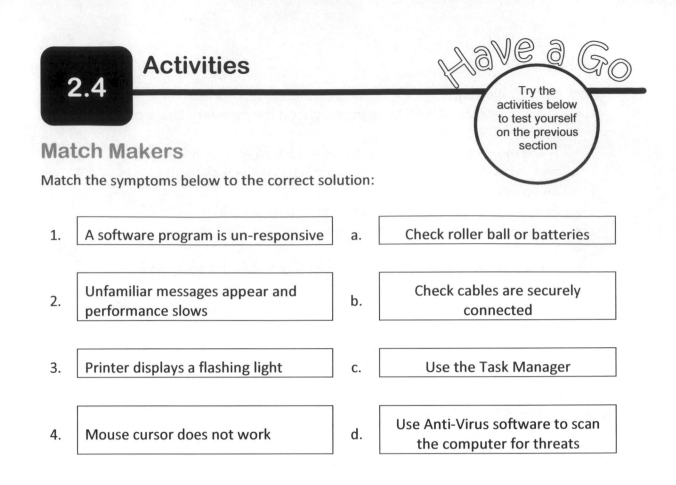

1.	A software program is un-responsive	a.	Check roller ball or batteries
2.	Unfamiliar messages appear and performance slows	b.	Check cables are securely connected
3.	Printer displays a flashing light	c.	Use the Task Manager
4.	Mouse cursor does not work	d.	Use Anti-Virus software to scan the computer for threats

Enter your answers below (e.g. 1a etc):

1.	
2.	
3.	
4.	

As Easy As....

A B C

1. Which of the following should be included on a reporting form?

A	Date and time of ICT problem	☐
B	Details of steps taken to resolve problem	☐
C	Error message names or codes	☐
D	All of the above	☐

Computer Viruses

Did You Know?

Anti-virus software should be updated regularly

> **NOTE:** this section contains crossover material from Level 1

Viruses

A virus is a malicious threat designed to harm your computer and computer data.

To guard against viruses it is important to install anti-virus software and regularly scan your computer and drives for threats.

New viruses are being created every day which is why it is important to update your anti-virus software regularly.

Examples of anti-virus software are:

- Norton Antivirus
- McAfee Antivirus
- AVG
- Kapersky Antivirus Security

Anti-virus software will scan your computer for threats and then either quarantine potential threats for later deletion or remove them (*disinfect*). There are many computer threats that can harm your computer; collectively they are referred to as 'malware' or malicious software. A **firewall** should also be installed to prevent unauthorised access to a computer system (called *hacking*).

Trojan Horses

A Trojan Horse is malicious software that is hidden so that it appears safe but allows a hacker unauthorised remote access to a user's computer. Trojan Horses can be downloaded unwittingly whilst downloading software or downloading ActiveX content from a website or via email attachments and can be used in identity theft.

Worms

A worm is a self replicating virus that can be downloaded and then passed on to other users via email attachments or network connections.

Spyware

Spyware is malicious software downloaded onto a user's computer which is used to monitor keystrokes and web browsing activities of the user. Anti-Spyware software should be installed to prevent spyware being downloaded onto a user's computer.

Adware

Adware refers to a program that displays advertising on a user's computer, usually in the form of 'pop-ups'. Adware advertising is designed to target the user and based on results from spyware monitoring of a user's web browsing habits.

Match Makers

Match the items below to the correct description:

1.	Worm	a.	malicious software that is hidden so that it appears safe but allows a hacker unauthorised remote access to a user's computer
2.	Trojan	b.	malicious software downloaded onto a user's computer which is used to monitor keystrokes and web browsing activities of the user
3.	Spyware	c.	prevents unauthorised access to a computer system
4.	Firewall	d.	A self replicating virus usually passed to other users via email or network connections

Enter your answers below (e.g. 1a etc):

1.	
2.	
3.	
4.	

As Easy As....

1. Adware displays advertising on a user's computer in which form?

A	Pop outs	☐
B	Pop ups	☐
C	Pop ins	☐
D	Pop ads	☐

Section 3 ▶

Using ICT

Save

Manage Information Storage to Enable Efficient Retrieval

THE MANCHESTER COLLEGE
COLLEGE LIBRARIES
ASHTON OLD ROAD
MANCHESTER
M11 2WH

Manage Information Storage

Did You Know?

Files deleted from the hard drive can be restored from the Recycle Bin

Managing files means saving files with meaningful names and storing them in a relevant location, such as on a drive or folder. Stored information may be:

- A mail merge letter created using a word processing application
- A report stored in a database
- A sales analysis created using a spreadsheet
- A looping slide show created using presentation software

The Importance of File Extensions

A good filename is one that is descriptive, enabling the user to recognise and identify the file – for example: **Invoice_33_Qualiteach_02Sep10**. A file is saved with a file extension to indicate the type of application in which it is saved:

- DOCX is the file extension for Microsoft® Office Word files
- XLSX is the file extension for Microsoft® Office Excel files
- ACCDB is the file extension for Microsoft® Office Access files
- PPTX is the file extension for Microsoft® Office PowerPoint files

When renaming a file it is important to enter the correct file extension so that the application can recognise the file. Opening a file with a missing or incorrect file extension will result in an error message. The file **Hobbies.docx** below is a Microsoft Word document (note the icon denotes the type of application).When renamed without the file extension, the file icon displays as an unrecognisable file type:

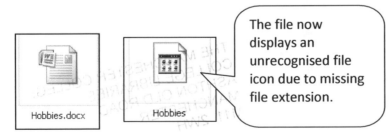

Hobbies.docx

Hobbies

The file now displays an unrecognised file icon due to missing file extension.

Folders

A folder is used to store files. A folder can contain many sub-folders (a sub-folder is a folder within a folder). A folder system stores files in a logical way and makes them easier to find.

Sales

Delivery

Invoices

3 folders, the main folder is called **Sales** and contains 2 further sub-folders, **Delivery** in which to store delivery notes and **Invoices** in which to store sales invoices

Compressing files

Compressing a file makes it a smaller size (compressed) to make it easier to store, download or send via email. When a file is compressed it is referred to as a *zipped* file. There are various compression software packages around, some of which can be downloaded for a limited period before being purchased. WinZip and WinRar are examples of this type of software. Folders cannot be emailed unless zipped first and some email applications will not accept email messages with database files attached; when zipped into a compressed folder the attachment will be accepted. More than one file can be compressed in one zipped folder. Large files such as videos and photographs can be reduced in size to make them more manageable once compressed.

Files can be un-compressed or unzipped by the recipient.

Zipped (compressed) folder

Recycle Bin

The Recycle Bin is positioned on the desktop and contains files which have been deleted from the hard drive of the computer. If necessary, deleted files can be restored to their original stored position. Files deleted from a removable storage device, such as a CD-RW or memory stick, and files deleted from network drives cannot be restored from the Recycle Bin.

Recycle Bin (full)   Recycle Bin (empty)

File and Folder Sizes

Files and folders containing files are measured in bytes (8 bits or **binary digits** to a byte), kilobytes, megabytes and gigabytes etc. Storage devices are also measured in bytes, so a file measuring 800 megabytes will not fit onto a Compact Disk (CD-RW), which is capable of holding up to 700 mb. An average Word document containing one page of text may only measure 30-50 kb whilst a computer program may measure much more than this (measured in megabytes or gigabytes).

- Kilobyte – 1024 bytes
- Megabyte - 1024 kilobytes
- Gigabyte - 1024 megabytes
- Terabyte – 1024 gigabytes

File Details

Microsoft Windows displays file sizes and other attributes of saved files, such as file type and date modified, within the Documents window.

	Burn	New folder				

Documents library				Arrange by:	Folder ▾
Functional Skills Updates 2010					
Name ▲		Date modified	Type		Size
2010 FS ICT Level 2 Activity Workbook do...		24/02/2011 12:02	Microsoft Word D...		6,
2010_FS_ICT_Level_2_Activity_Workbook_...		24/02/2011 10:34	WinZip File		5,

 © Lorna Bointon, Qualiteach Education 2014

File Properties

The properties of a file including file name, file size, file type, file location, date created, date modified and date accessed can be found in the File Properties dialog box.

File attributes can also be selected from this dialog box, such as Read-only. The Read-only file attribute ensures that users can open the file but not make changes to it.

File properties can be viewed and attributes can be selected, such as Read-only, by selecting the tick boxes

The file name is followed by [Read-only]

If a user attempts to amend and save the file with the same name a message appears:

'Teddy.xlsx' is read-only. To save a copy, click OK, then give the workbook a new name in the Save As dialog box.

In order to save their changes, the user must save a copy of the file with a new name.

   © Lorna Bointon, Qualiteach Education 2014

Storage Devices

Did You Know?

Data should be backed up onto portable media and kept off-site

Storage devices are devices on which you can save and store files and folders. A computer contains a hard drive, usually called the C: or Local Drive which is built-in to the computer (although some hard drives can be installed externally). Other storage devices are removable and can be used to transfer data between computers or used as backing storage.

Backing up data is important in the event of disk or drive failure or fire, theft or corruption.

Hard disks

Hard disks can be internal within the base unit or an external storage device. The hard drive stores the programs on the computer and is capable of storing a large amount of data.

Portable Media

Portable media refers to any storage device not built in to the computer which can be used to back up important files or transfer data between computers. Portable media is also referred to as *removable storage* and includes the following:

- CD-RW – Compact Disc (Read/Write) capable of holding up to 700 mb of data and commonly used to store data and audio files

- DVD-RW – used to hold film and movie files a Digital Versatile Disc is capable of holding up to 4.70 GB (single layer) or up to 17.08 GB for a double sided, dual layer.

- USB Memory Stick or Flash Drive – used for flash drives/memory sticks. Solid state technology means that there are no spinning or moving parts contained in a USB device. This removable and portable device is inserted into a USB port to store and transfer data between computers

- SD Card – a Secure Digital device used in portable devices, such as laptop computers

- Floppy disks – an outdated removable storage device capable of storing up to 1.44 mb of data, can be prone to corruption.

- Network Drive – this is a shared drive used by client computers on a shared network and served by a computer called the *server*. Network drives are usually password protected against deletion, editing or unauthorised access.

 © Lorna Bointon, Qualiteach Education 2014

Online (Virtual) Storage

Remote backup services are provided by ISPs over Broadband Internet connections, providing convenient access to files over the Internet and ability to share files with friends, family or colleagues, via a password. It also allows a user to protect files by enabling automatic backup. For data security reasons, this form of storage is not recommended for confidential or sensitive data

Sharing Files (Google Apps)

Sharing files with other users online is made possible by using file sharing software, such as Google Docs. This application enables users to share and edit documents, spreadsheets and presentations at the same time. Files can be stored and shared using online storage.

 © Lorna Bointon, Qualiteach Education 2014

Save a file to a removable storage device

- Right click the file and choose **Send To**. From the sub menu, select the removable storage drive.

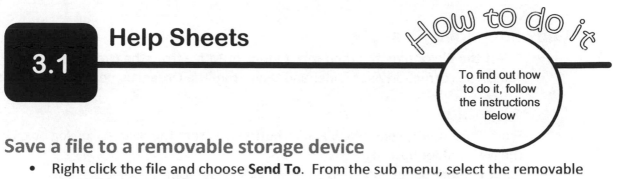

Send To ▶	📖 Compressed (zipped) Folder
Cut	🖼 Desktop (create shortcut)
Copy	📄 Mail Recipient
Create Shortcut	📁 My Documents
Delete	🖳 Share-to-Web Upload Folder
Rename	Ⓢ Skype
Properties	💾 3½ Floppy (A:)
	💿 CD-RW Drive (F:)
	💾 Removable (G:)
	💾 Removable (H:)

Compress/zip a file or files

- Select the file or files (to select multiple non-adjacent files, hold down the **CTRL** key whilst clicking each file to select them)
- Right click and choose **Send To**. From the sub-menu choose **Compressed (Zipped) Folder.**

Uncompress/unzip a file

- Right click the zipped folder and choose **Extract All**.

- The Extraction Wizard will start. Follow the steps, clicking **Next** between each step, in the wizard to choose the location in which to extract the files (use the **Browse** button to find the correct drive and folder). Click **Finish**.

Rename files and folders

- In Documents, right click the file and choose **Rename**
- Enter the new name (ensure that a file retains the correct file extension)
- Press Enter or click away from the file

Delete files and folders

- Select the file or folder and then press the **Delete** key on the keyboard
- Confirm deletion by clicking **Yes**

Restore files from the Recycle Bin

- Double click the Recycle Bin icon. Select the file to be restored and then click **Restore this Item**. The file will be restored to its original location.

Copy and move files

- Select the file or files and then select **Copy** or **Move** from the **Organize** menu
- Select the correct drive or folder and then, from the **Organize** menu, select **Paste**

Create a folder

- From Documents, select **New Folder** button *OR* From the **Save As** dialog box, click the **New Folder** button
- Enter a folder name and press Enter or click away from the folder

View File attributes

- From the Documents window select the **View** arrow and choose **Details.**

- File details such as file name, file size, file type and date modified will be displayed.

Name	Date modified	Type	Size
2010 FS ICT Level 2 Activity Workbook do...	24/02/2011 12:15	Microsoft Word D...	6,429 KB
2010_FS_ICT_Level_2_Activity_Workbook_...	24/02/2011 10:34	WinZip File	5,977 KB

Change File Properties

- Right click the file and choose **Properties.**

- The File Properties dialog box opens. To ensure that a user cannot modify and save the file with the same name, select the Read-only tick box and click OK.

- To remove the Read-only attribute, re-enter the Properties dialog box and remove the tick from the tick box. Click OK.

Insert a Memory Stick

- Find the USB port, either at the front or back of the computer (there is usually more than one USB port on a PC). Uncap the memory stick and insert carefully into the USB port. Check to see if the Removable drive is listed with the other drives in Computer.

Safely Remove hardware (Memory Stick)

- To safely remove the memory stick from the USB port, select the Safely Remove Hardware icon on the Task Bar. Select the relevant device from the dialog box and click Stop. Await the Windows safety notification before unplugging your device

Insert a CD/DVD

- Press the button on the front of the CD or DVD drive; the tray will slide out. Place the CD or DVD onto the tray and press the button again to slide it in and close the drive.

 © Lorna Bointon, Qualiteach Education 2014

Match Makers

1. Match the correct answer with the question below:

1.	Creates reduced file size	a	Gigabyte
2.	Restores deleted files	b	File extension
3.	Equivalent to 1024 megabytes	c	Compressed (zipped) file
4.	Indicates file type	d	Recycle Bin

Enter your answers below (e.g. 1a etc):

1.		2.		3.		4.	

2. Match the correct answer with the question below:

1.	Stores the computer's programs	a	CD-RW
2.	This is a secure digital device used in laptop computers	b	DVD
3.	Stores film and movie files and has single or double dual layers	c	SD Card
4.	Stores audio files and can hold up to 700mb	d	Hard Drive

Enter your answers below (e.g. 1a etc):

1.		2.		3.		4.	

 © Lorna Bointon, Qualiteach Education 2014

As Easy As....

1. Which of the following statements about portable storage is correct?

A	Enables remote, online storage	☐
B	A shared drive, usually password protected	☐
C	Holds computer programs	☐
D	Inserts into a USB port to store and transfer data between computers	☐

2. Which of the following statements about the Recycle Bin is *incorrect*?

A	A file deleted from a memory stick can be restored to its original location	☐
B	A file deleted from the hard drive can be restored to its original location	☐
C	The Recycle Bin icon is usually positioned on the Desktop	☐
D	The Recycle Bin icon changes to show that it contains files or is empty	☐

3. Which of the following statements about compressing files is correct?

A	File compression reduces file size	☐
B	File compression increases file size	☐
C	File compression does not affect file size	☐
D	File compression can only be used on large files, such as videos	☐

4. Which of the following file attributes will ensure that users cannot save a file with the same name?

A	Hidden	☐
B	Write only	☐
C	Read-only	☐
D	Read-Write	☐

 © Lorna Bointon, Qualiteach Education 2014

Practice Makes Perfect

3.1

Practical Exercise 1

1. Create a folder called **Charity Jump**

2. Within the **Charity Jump** folder, create 2 further sub-folders named **Promote** and **Budget**

3. Open Microsoft® Word and a new document. Enter the heading **CHARITY TEDDY PARACHUTE JUMP.** Save this document as **Teddy_jump.docx** within the **Promote** folder.

4. Close the **Teddy_jump** document. Open Microsoft® Excel and a new spreadsheet.

5. Save the spreadsheet as **jump_costs.xlsx** in the **Budget** folder.

6. Close **jump_costs.xlsx**

Practical Exercise 2

1. Rename the **Promote** folder as **Adverts**

2. Rename the **Teddy_jump** document as **parachute_jump.docx**

3. Copy the **jump_costs** spreadsheet into the **Adverts** folder

4. Delete the **jump_costs** spreadsheet from the **Budget** folder

5. Move the **jump_costs** spreadsheet from the **Adverts** folder into the **Budget** folder

Practical Exercise 3

1. Make the **parachute_jump** document read-only

2. Re-save the document as **charity_jump** into the **Adverts** folder so that there are two copies of the file with different files names

3. Delete the **parachute_ jump** document from the **Adverts** folder

4. Restore the **parachute_jump** document from the Recycle Bin (this will only work if the file is saved on the hard drive).

Practical Exercise 4

1. Display details for the files saved in the **Adverts** folder and make a note of the file sizes. The Adverts folder containing the two files should measure no more 24 kb.

2. Compress (zip) the **Adverts** folder and note the reduced file size (should be around 18kb).

3. Back up the Charity Jump folder onto a removable storage device.

 © Lorna Bointon, Qualiteach Education 2014

Section 4 ▶

Finding and Selecting Information

Find

Use appropriate search techniques to locate and select relevant information

The Internet

Did You Know?

Each computer is connected to the Internet via a unique IP address

NOTE: See the **Level 1** Functional Skills Activity Workbook and Revision Guide for background information on the Internet, ISPs, different types of Internet connectivity and the World Wide Web

The Internet is a global network of interconnected computers, which communicate via unique IP addresses (Internet Protocol).

The World Wide Web (WWW) is a collection of web pages on the Internet which can be accessed via search engines or a specific URL

The Internet is referred to as the Information Super Highway. A language called Transmission Control Protocol /Internet Protocol (Protocol means language) TCP/IP is used to communicate in a universal language that each computer can understand. To enable fast transfer of files over the Internet **FTP** is used (FTP means **File Transfer Protocol**). The **Home Page** in a website is the first page of a set of web pages and contains links to various pages within that site, and sometimes links to other pages on the World Wide Web. The Internet is programmed using **HTML** (Hypertext Mark-up Language).

The Internet can be used for online banking, booking tickets, communicating via social networks or chat rooms, downloading music and videos, reference sites for education, shopping and bidding in online auctions.

A web browser is needed in order to use the Internet, such as Firefox, Internet Explorer or Google Chrome.

URL

A specific web address is called a URL (uniform Resource Locator) and is entered into the Address Bar to find a specific website. All website addresses start with **http://** which is automatically entered at the front of the address and stands for **Hypertext Transfer Protocol** (protocol means language). The next part of the website address is **www.** followed by the **domain name** –usually the company name and then **co.uk, ac.uk, .com, .org, .net, .gov** indicate the type of organisation or the location of the server. See the example below:

All web addresses or URLs start with Http:// (stands for Hypertext Transfer Protocol and this is entered automatically)

http://www.google.co.uk

World Wide Web

The domain name and geographical location

Search Engines

If you do not have access to the specific URL of a website you will need to use a search engine. A search engine is an Internet search tool which is designed to search within its vast database for specified keywords or phrases (called search criteria) entered by a user into a search engine box. A list of web page links that match the keywords, in order of relevance, will be displayed. When clicked, a webpage link will open a webpage which contains one or more of the keywords. A website designer will enter Meta tags which are descriptive words designed to ensure that the website is found.

Search criteria may be a single keyword or a phrase. To ensure that the whole phrase (or string) is found, the keywords should be entered within quotation marks, e.g. "Irish Wolfhound".

The keywords **Irish Wolfhound** without quotation marks will result in pages being found that include **Irish** or **Wolfhound**, whereas enclosing the keywords ensures that only pages containing the phrase **Irish Wolfhound** will be listed.

Examples of search engines include:

Google	**www.google.com or www.google.co.uk**
Yahoo	**www.yahoo.com**
AltaVista	**www.altavista.com**
Excite	**www.excite.com**
Lycos	**www.lycos.com**
Ask Jeeves	**www.ask.com**
MSN	**www.msn.com**

Local Search Engines

Large websites use local search engines which are designed to find information within the site.

Subject Directories

Most search engines contain a subject directory. These are lists of subject categories that, when selected, take you to another list of sub-categories. Google contains a Directory in

http://www.google.com/intl/en/options/.

Organising Bookmarks

The webpage link can be saved, so that it can be accessed later, by adding the page to **Favorites**. This is called *bookmarking* a web page. Favorites can be organised within folders, making them easier to locate and open.

For example, three webpage links have been organised within a folder called **Build-up Ex L2:**

Search Techniques

Did You Know?

The wildcard* symbol can be used in place of characters in a search word

Advanced Search Techniques and Boolean Operators (AND, OR, NOT)

Search engines use a database to hold vast amounts of information which can be queried by entering keywords into a search engine box.

For example, entering *cat* into a search engine will result in many web pages containing this keyword being found. To refine or narrow down a search, a user can do the following:

- Use Boolean operators, such as + (AND), - (NOT), OR. Excluding words can be an effective way of narrowing down a search, for example excluding the word *Thailand* from the search (Korat –Thailand) will find web pages relating to Korat cats and not the city in Thailand.

Some search engines use AND/NOT whereas others use + and – (Google uses OR, + and -).

AND operator

The AND operator or + will find pages that include both keywords used in the search. For example **Aberdaron AND Bardsey Island** (or **Aberdaron +Bardsey Island**) will include both sets of criteria in the search results.

OR operator

The OR operator will find pages that include at least one of the keywords used in the search. For example **Aberdaron OR Bardsey Island** will include pages that relate to one or both sets of criteria in the search results. So you will see pages that include information about Aberdaron, pages containing information on Bardsey Island and pages that will display information on both sets of criteria.

NOT operator

The NOT or – operator is used to exclude words from a search. For example, **Aberdaron NOT Bardsey Island** (or Aberdaron–Bardsey Island).

Wildcards *%

Another search tool is the **wildcard ***. This can be used in place of characters within a word. For example, specif* will find **specify, specified, specific, specifically** etc. To replace only one character in the search keyword, use the % symbol (e.g. **specifi%** will find **specific** but not specifically or specify/specified).

Using Advanced Search Engine Features

Narrow down a search by using the Advanced Search facility in a search engine, such as Google, to do the following:

In the example below, Fiat is added in the **All these words** box. Three Fiat models are added to the **One or more of these words**. **Panda** is excluded from the search. English is the search language and UK is the region chosen. The pages will be as recent as the last 24 hours. The numeric range that is being searched is between £800 and £1500.

Find web pages that have...

all these words:	Fiat
this exact wording or phrase:	
one or more of these words:	Cinquecento OR 100 OR Punto

But don't show pages that have...

any of these unwanted words:	Panda

Need more tools?

Results per page:	10 results
Language:	English
File type:	any format
Search within a site or domain:	

(e.g. youtube.com, .edu)

⊟ Date, usage rights, numeric range, and more

Date: (how recent the page is)	past 24 hours
Usage rights:	not filtered by license
Where your keywords show up:	anywhere in the page
Region:	United Kingdom
Numeric range:	800 .. 1500

(e.g. $1500..$3000)

SafeSearch: ◉ Off ○ On

[Advanced Search]

- Specify a make of car, e.g. Fiat
- Exclude words, e.g. Panda
- Specify a date that the page was last updated (within last week or 24 hours)
- Specify the region as UK with English as the language
- Specify a numeric range (e.g. only show cars between £800 and £1500)

Make of car (e.g. **Fiat**)	Model (e.g. **NOT** Panda	Specify when updated	Specify region	Numeric range
				£0-£0

   © Lorna Bointon, Qualiteach Education 2014

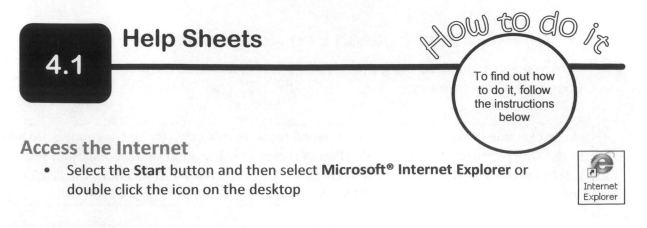

Access the Internet

- Select the **Start** button and then select **Microsoft® Internet Explorer** or double click the icon on the desktop

Internet Explorer

Enter a URL

- Click the cursor into the Address Bar at the top of the web page and enter the URL.

http://www.google.co.uk/

- Press Enter or click the green arrow to go to the URL or click the X to stop the page from downloading.

Use a Search Engine

- Click the cursor into the search box and enter the search criteria, i.e. keyword or phrase.
- Press the Enter key or click the **Search** button (if using Google™ UK, click **Google Search)**.
- A list of web pages will be displayed in order of relevance. Click a link to see the web page.
- Click **Advanced Search** to refine your search further. *Advanced Search*

Bookmark a webpage

- Select the **Favorites** button and then click the **Add to Favorites** button.
- The **Add to Favorites** dialog box appears. Choose a folder from the **Create In** drop down menu. Enter a name or keep the existing name and click **Add.**
- To see a list of stored web page links, select the **Favorites** button — ☆ Favorites
- Click a Favorite link to open the web page — 🌐 Functional skills standards →

Organise Favorites

- Select the **Favorites** button and then click the **Add to Favorites** arrow. Select **Organize Favorites** from the menu.
- Select the **New Folder** button, enter a folder name
- Select an existing webpage link and click **Move** to move it to a new folder. Double click the folder name and click OK. Click **Close**.

Perform an Advanced Search

- Click **Advanced Search** to refine your search further. Advanced Search
- Enter the keywords in the **All these words** box or enter an exact wording pr phrase
- To use the **OR** operator, enter keywords into the **One or more of these words** boxes
- To exclude words, enter them into the **Any of these unwanted words** box
- In the **Need more Tools** section, Select the amount of results you want to see per page
- Choose a language and file type (for example if you only want to see PDF files)
- Select a specific website or domain in which to search
- Click the **Date, usage rights, numeric range and more** link to expand it. Select the date the webpage was last updated (to ensure currency), the usage rights (copyright, licence free etc) and where the keyword will show up (e.g. anywhere on the page)
- Choose a region to narrow the search.
- Enter a numeric range (e.g. between 1000 and 2000)
- Click **Advanced Search**

Find web pages that have...	
all these words:	Fiat
this exact wording or phrase:	tip
one or more of these words:	Cinquecento OR 100 OR Punto tip
But don't show pages that have...	
any of these unwanted words:	Panda tip
Need more tools?	
Results per page:	10 results
Language:	English
File type:	any format
Search within a site or domain:	
	(e.g. youtube.com, .edu)
⊖ Date, usage rights, numeric range, and more	
Date: (how recent the page is)	past 24 hours
Usage rights:	not filtered by license
Where your keywords show up:	anywhere in the page
Region:	United Kingdom
Numeric range:	800 .. 1500
	(e.g. $1500..$3000)
SafeSearch:	◉ Off ◯ On
	Advanced Search

Using the Find Tool in Microsoft® Internet Explorer

- Select the **Edit** menu and then select **Find on this page** (if the menu bar is missing, hold down the **Alt** key) or press **Ctrl** and **F** to see the Find bar.

- Enter the search criteria within the **Find** box and click **Next**. Continue clicking **Next** until each occurrence of the search word has been found.

✕ Find:	Functional Skills	Previous Next

 © Lorna Bointon, Qualiteach Education 2014

Activities

Match Makers

Match the correct answers to the questions below:

1.	This can be used to replace a single character in a search word	a	*
2.	These are used to contain search words and refine a search	b	%
3.	This can be used to replace more than one character in a search	c.	+ and -
4.	These are Boolean operators	d.	" "

Enter your answers below:

1.		2.		3.		4.	

As Easy As....

1. The search criteria **cats + dogs –rabbits** would result in which of the following?

A	Links to pages containing the search words cats or dogs or rabbits	☐
B	Links to pages including the search words cats and dogs but excluding rabbits	☐
C	Links to pages including the search word rabbits but not cats or dogs	☐
D	Links to pages including the search word cats and dogs and rabbits	☐

 © Lorna Bointon, Qualiteach Education 2014

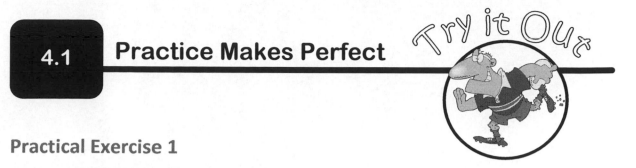

4.1 Practice Makes Perfect

Practical Exercise 1

1. Access the Internet

2. Enter the URL **www.google.co.uk** in the Address Bar

3. Using the Google UK search engine find information on **"bardsey island"**, using the keywords and quotation marks as shown

4. Refine the search further by entering **OR Aberdaron**

5. Ensure that the keywords **fishing trips, boat trips** and **day trips** are excluded from the search.

6. Ensure that the search will only show pages that have been updated in the last month

7. Ensure that the search will only find UK web pages using the English language

Practical Exercise 2

1. Using a Google search engine, perform another search to find information on broadband providers and prices. Refine the search by doing the following:

    o Exclude AOL

    o Search UK only

    o Ensure that web page information was updated within the last week

    o Find broadband providers with prices between £10 and £15 per month.

Practical Exercise 3

1. Go to **en.wikipedia.org** and use the internal search engine to find information on *Boolean Operators*

2. Check to see when the page was last modified or updated

3. Check for information about copyright (Terms of Use)

4. Check that the information is relevant.

5. Use a search engine to find another source of information about Boolean Operators.

6. Find a relevant webpage and bookmark it.

Important: to provide proof of Internet searches, and other tasks which cannot be printed normally, you will need to create screen prints: press the **Print Screen** key (to copy the whole screen) or the **Alt** key and the **Print Screen** key together (to copy a dialog box). Paste the screen print in a Microsoft Word document and save.

© Lorna Bointon, Qualiteach Education 2014

Section 5 ▶
Finding and Selecting Information

Select information from a variety of sources to meet
requirements of a complex task

Select Information

Information sources also include texting and social networks

Complex Tasks

The types of task that requires information from a variety of sources include:

- Creating a multi-page report on sales performance

  - Spreadsheet or other financial data, graphs and charts, images, performance analysis of sales representatives, comparisons with previous year's performance

- Creating a presentation about saving our coastlines and aquatic life

  - The internet, environmental magazines or encyclopaedias for information and facts, images and photographs, graphs to chart costal erosion and other environmental issues

- Creating a newsletter to go out to subscribers of a charity

  - Information about events from area organisers, charts showing profits made, information relating to the charity, interviews or quotes from people involved in fund raising, images and photos, a database of names and addresses of subscribers

Information Sources

Although the Internet is an easy to access and varied source of information, there are many other non-ICT based information sources available:

Non-ICT Information Sources
- Newspapers, magazines, books
- Images, diagrams, maps
- Conversations, text messages

ICT Information sources:
- CDs and DVDs (encyclopaedias, documentaries, language courses)
- Websites such as wikis, podcasts, weblogs (blogs), web-based reference sites (webopaedias)
- Databases, spreadsheets, reports

 © Lorna Bointon, Qualiteach Education 2014

Copyright ©

Some sources of information are subject to Copyright law which safeguards the copyright owner's interests. Copyright law ensures that text, audio, video; music, song lyrics or images belonging to the copyright owner (usually the creator/writer or publisher) cannot be copied without the copyright owner's consent. Copyright of literary, artistic and musical work lasts for 70 years from the death of a known author or 70 years from creation of the work, if the author is unknown. Check for copyright by looking for the following symbol © and any copyright information that has been provided on the website. If in doubt contact the copyright owner for permission. Unauthorised copying and sharing of text, images or music is illegal. Copyright law also relates to computer software programs and a licence is required before copyrighted software can be installed. The Digital Economy Act 2010 regulates digital media and has been implemented to prevent online copyright infringement and the infringement of performers' rights. This act allows the secretary of state to ensure that Internet service providers block access to or limit service to an Internet site that has engaged in illegal sharing or copyright infringement.

Plagiarism means passing off someone else's work as your own. Always get permission first before copying or downloading text, images or music and acknowledge sources of information.

Fitness for Purpose

It is important to make sure that the information used in complex tasks is fit for purpose. This means making sure that the information is up-to-date, is factual rather than containing a one-sided opinion or hearsay not based on fact and that it is relevant to the task.

Before using information it is important to evaluate the following:

Currency

It is important that information is up-to-date and current. To check the currency of information, always look for a date that the website was last updated.

To ensure that only up-to-date websites are found and listed, use an advanced search to select a timeframe in which the website was last updated (last 24 hours, last week etc).

Relevance

Keywords entered into a search engine may result in many web pages being found. Some of the web pages may contain the keyword but may not be relevant to your search. For example, entering 'hotspot' into a search engine may result in pages relating to WIFI hotspots being found but also pages on holiday hotspots or geological hotspots.

Bias

Bias is a one-sided opinion or view which may contain prejudice and not be based on fact. To gain a balanced view of a topic, it is important to check that information is not presented entirely from one point of view. Be careful about using wiki sites, such as Wikipedia, without cross-referencing with other sites of information as wikis are edited directly from a users computer.

    © Lorna Bointon, Qualiteach Education 2014

Match Makers

Match the correct answers to the questions below:

1.	Lasts for 70 years after owner's death	a	Plagiarism
2.	Copying and passing off someone else's work as your own	b	Currency
3.	A one sided view not based on fact	c	Copyright
4.	Check for this to ensure information is up-to-date	d	Bias

Enter your answers below:

1.		2.		3.		4.	

As Easy As....

1. Which of the following is **not** a constraint on the use of information?

A	Plagiarism	☐
B	Copyright	☐
C	Software licence	☐
D	Collaborative editing	☐

2. Checking for fitness of purpose involves evaluating which of the following?

A	Bias	☐
B	Currency	☐
C	Relevance	☐
D	All of the above	☐

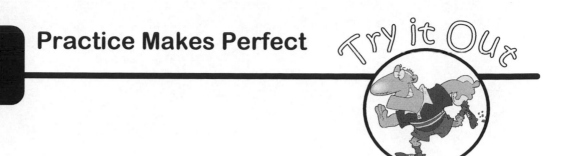

Practical Exercise 1

1.   Using the Internet find information about marine life in Cardigan Bay west Wales

2.   Find a site that includes information and pictures about dolphins

3.   Check when the website was last updated and check to see if there is a copyright symbol

4.   Now use the Internet to find copyright and royalty free images of dolphins

4.   Save a picture of a dolphin (right click image and select **Save Picture As**)

Practical Exercise 2

1.   Use a non-ICT source to find information about marine conservation in the UK

2.   List the sources that you have used, explain why you have used your chosen information source and whether the information is fit for purpose

3.   List a further three sources of information you could have used

Practical Exercise 3

1.   Explain the difference between copyright and plagiarism

2.   Explain why it is important to check information sources for bias, currency and relevance

Note: for the practice assessments and the actual exam, you will be supplied with a source record sheet on which to record sources of information, such as website addresses.

Section 6 ▸

Developing, Presenting and Communicating Information

Edit

Enter, develop and refine information using appropriate software to meet the requirements of a complex task

Apply Editing, Formatting and Layout Techniques

Did You KNow?

A complex task may require various software applications

Note: For basic formatting techniques, such as fonts, sizes, colour, alignment etc, see the **Level 1** Functional Skills Activity Workbook and Revision Guide

Editing Techniques

Finding Information

Searches can be achieved by using the find facility in Microsoft® Office applications. The **Find** tool is common to each of the Microsoft® Office applications and is used to find part or whole words or phrases within a document.

Replacing Information

Manually replacing a word with another word throughout a multi-page document would be tedious and time consuming and errors could be made, resulting in some words not being replaced. Using the Replace facility in Microsoft Office® is a more time efficient method which enables replacement of one or more words with replacement word(s) in one action. The Replace facility allows the user to search for specified text, either whole words or partial text, and then replace it with different specified text. For example, the word 'cat' can be replaced by the word 'feline' wherever it occurs within a document, but care should be taken to search for whole words only or it could result in words containing the search characters 'cat', such as cathartic, catamaran, catapult, scatological etc, also being included in the Replace action.

Selecting Information

Data within a document must first be selected before it can be formatted. Selection, also referred to as 'highlighting', can be achieved using a variety of methods such as mouse, keyboard or ribbon command. Selected data is displayed with shading or 'highlighting'.

Show and Hide Characters

To see non-printing characters on a page, such as page breaks, section breaks and paragraph marks, the **Show/Hide** button can be used. See examples below:

¶	Paragraph return
°	Non-breaking space (or protected space)
↵	Soft carriage return or soft line break
→	Tab
....	Spaces
·······Page Break·······	Page break

Document Layout

Different layout techniques that can be applied to information include the following:

- **Margins** are the space between the edge of the paper and the text on the page. left, right, top and bottom page margins can be increased or decreased
- **Headers and footers** are information that appear at the top and/or bottom of each of the pages in a document, including dates, numbering, filenames or author name
- **Page numbering** can be applied automatically to the top or bottom of a document, spreadsheet, report or slide. Page numbers will automatically display in sequential order for each page. Page numbers can be formatted to appear as Roman Numerals or letters, e.g. i, ii, iii or a, b, c etc
- **Orientation** refers to the layout of a page. The default orientation of a document, database or spreadsheet is portrait. *Portrait* is taller and narrower than *Landscape*
- **Page breaks**. A *soft* page break is automatically inserted when text reaches the end of a page and needs to continue on a separate page. A *hard* page break is inserted by the user wherever a new page is required.
- **Section breaks** are used to break a document or page into sections
- **Columns** are used for newspaper style documents where text flows from the end of one column to the top of the next column
- **Tabs** are used to position text and numbers in parallel columns. Numbers can be aligned by using decimal tab styles
- **Paragraph spacing** is applied to ensure consistency of spacing between paragraphs without using the Enter key to create spaces
- **Indentation** creates a space between the left and/or right margins and paragraphs or other data
- **Vertical alignment** is applied to align data vertically on the page. The default vertical alignment in a document is **Top.**
- **Text direction** is applied to text to display it at varying degrees

Formatting Techniques

Formatting techniques which can be used to enhance the presentation of a document include the following:

- **Styles** are applied to ensure consistency in a document
- **Tables** are used to organise and display data within rows and columns
- **Multi-level numbering** is applied to paragraphs, such as in legal documents
- **Paragraph borders** and **shading** enhance text in a document
- Inserting **symbols and special characters** such as copyright ©
- Superscripts, subscripts and other font effects, such as ~~strikethrough,~~ outline
- **Change case**, such as Sentence case and UPPERCASE
- **Bullet styles** can be formatted in a different colour or style or as a picture
- **Copy Formatting** from one item of data to another

Business Letter Layout

A business letter is a formal type of correspondence which is presented on letter headed paper (e.g. the letter contains the company's name and address and logo at the top, side or bottom of the letter).

A letter should be dated, include the recipient's name and address (a recipient is someone who receives) and may include a subject line. The body of the letter should be written in concise, business language.

A letter addressed to a person by name, such as **Dear Mr Smith**, should end with **Yours sincerely**. The first part (Dear etc is called a *salutation* and the closing part of the letter is called a *complimentary close*). A letter addressed to Dear Sir or Madam should close with **Yours faithfully**.

At least 5 spaces should follow the complimentary close and the sender's name and position to allow for a signature.

If there is another document, cheque or other item enclosed with the letter this should be indicated by typing **Enc** or **Enc(s)** at least 2 spaces beneath the sender's name and position.

See the example below:

Qualiteach Education
Unit 36, Westminster Chambers
7 Hunter Street ◄----- Printed on letter headed paper
Chester
CH1 2HR
www.qualiteach.co.uk

Date ◄------------------------- - Letters should be dated

Recipient's name
Recipient's Address

Dear *Recipient Name* ◄------------------------- - Salutation

Order No: 1234 ◄------------------------- - Subject line

Thank you for ordering Fast Forward Functional Skills Information Communication Technology (ICT) Level 1.

We hope that you find it informative and helpful. I enclose a list of ◄----- Main body of letter using formal business language
further resources available for Functional Skills ICT.

Yours sincerely

Lorna Bointon ◄----- Complimentary close followed by 5 spaces for signature

Lorna Bointon
Author

Enc: Resource List ◄----- Indicates an enclosure with the letter

 © Lorna Bointon, Qualiteach Education 2014

Tables

Tables can be used in a variety of documents to hold text, numerical information, prices or images. Formulas can be added to a table to calculate totals and data can be sorted by one of more columns. An example of a document which uses one or more tables is an invoice:

Logo is inserted here

The address details are entered here

This is where the recipient's address is displayed

Order date, terms, due date here

This table is where the purchase order number, quantity, code, description, price and totals are entered

The text INVOICE is entered here

Invoice number and date here

This is where the shipping address is displayed if different

This is where the calculations are made

Make cheques payable to.....

Columns are merged

Borders and shading are used to define table areas

Templates

Templates are files that contain standard layout features which can be used repeatedly and then saved with a different filename. An example of a template is a blank invoice which has been set up with a specific layout, such as margins, line spacing, fonts, company logo and tables (see the invoice template above). Microsoft Office programs contain templates which the user can download and then adapt to their own preferences and save.

Multi-level Numbering

Multi-level numbering is applied to lists and paragraphs in documents, such as legal documents

Paragraph 1
1. Section
   1.1. Sub-section
      1.1.1. Sub-section

© Lorna Bointon, Qualiteach Education 2014

Columns

Columns are used within newsletters, folded adverts/leaflets and flyers. The examples below show the outside and inside pages of a three column, folded leaflet:

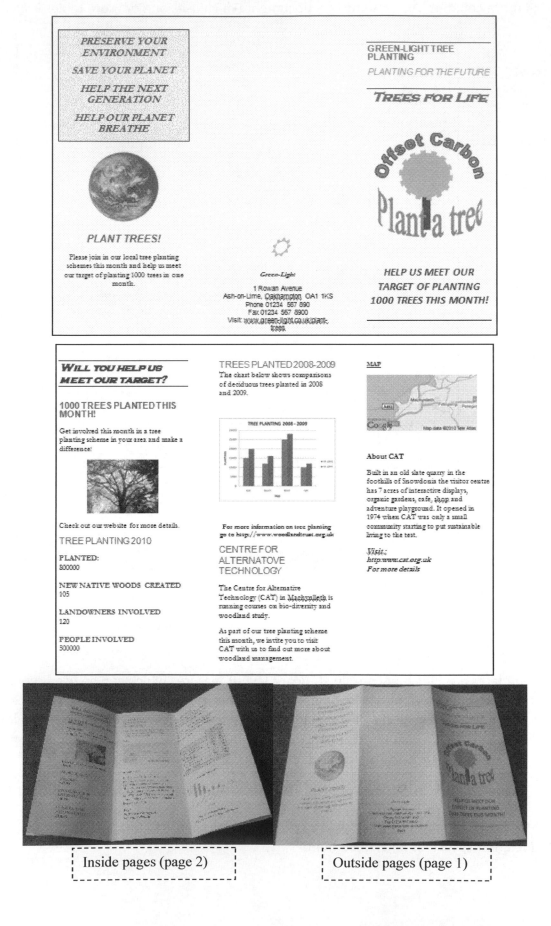

Inside pages (page 2)   Outside pages (page 1)

 © Lorna Bointon, Qualiteach Education 2014

Note: for basic editing techniques such as deleting, inserting and overtyping, see the **Level 1** Functional Skills Activity Workbook and Revision Guide

Editing Techniques

Selecting Text (Keyboard)

1 character to the right	Shift and →
1 character to the left	Shift and ←
1 word to the right	Shift and Ctrl and →
1 word to the left	Shift and ←
1 line of text	Shift and ↓
1 paragraph	Shift and CTRL and ↓
From cursor position to end of document	Shift and CTRL and End
From Cursor position to beginning of document	Shift and CTRL and Home
Whole document	CTRL and A

Selecting Text (Mouse)

1 word	Place cursor in word and double click
1 sentence	Place cursor at beginning of sentence and press CTRL and click
1 line	Place mouse pointer in left margin and click
1 paragraph	Place mouse pointer in left margin and double click or place cursor within text and treble-click
Multiple paragraphs	Place mouse arrow into left margin, click and drag over required paragraphs
Whole document	Place mouse in left margin and press CTRL and click

Selecting Text (Ribbon)

- To select all of the text in the document, select the **Select** arrow from the **Home** tab/**Editing** group and then choose **Select All**
- To select text with similar formatting, select this option from the **Select** drop down menu

Select

Select All

Select Objects

Select Text with Similar Formatting

Text Highlight Colour

- To apply *highlight* colour, select the **Text Highlight Color** arrow from the Font group and select a colour.

WordArt

- From the **Insert** tab, select **WordArt**. Click a WordArt style. Enter text into the dialog box and click OK. Select WordArt text to see the **Drawing Tools/Format** tab.

Insert or edit shapes or draw text box	Choose Shape styles	Change line and fill colour and shape effects	Add shadow or 3D effects	Change the position and text wrapping, alignment and rotation	Change height & width

Bullet Styles

- Highlight the list and then click the **Bullets** arrow from the **Home** tab and the **Paragraph** group.

- Choose a bullet style from the **Bullet Library** or click **Define New Bullet**

Select the **Symbol** button to change the bullet to a symbol, and the **Picture** button to use Clipart or 3D coloured bullet styles.

Use the **Font** button to change the font of the bullet

Change the bullet alignment from here

Define New Bullet

Bullet character

Symbol...   Picture...   Font...

Alignment:

Left

Preview

OK   Cancel

Multi-Level Numbering

- Highlight the text to be numbered. Select the **Multi-level List** arrow to see the **List Library**
- Choose a list or select **Define New List Level**
- Click a level to modify the number format, style, indent and alignment. Click OK.
- Change the list level of an existing list by selecting it and then, from the **Multi-level List** arrow, select **Change List Level** and select an option.

Superscripts and Subscripts

- A superscript displays above the normal line of text, e.g. 25^0C. To format text as superscript, select the **Superscript** command on the **Home** tab/**Font** group.
- The shortcut keyboard combination to apply superscript is **Ctrl** and **Shift** and **=**
- A subscript displays below the normal line of text, e.g. H_2O. To format text as subscript, select the **Subscript** command on the **Home** tab/**Font** group.
- The shortcut keyboard combination to apply subscript is **Ctrl** and **=**
- To remove character formatting, such as superscript or subscript, hold down **Ctrl** and press the **Spacebar**.

Font Effects

- From the **Home** tab, select the **Font** dialog box launcher icon and the **Font** dialog box will appear:
- Select an effect by clicking a tick box
- Superscripts and subscripts can also be applied from this dialog box

Effects		
Strikethrough	Shadow	Small caps
Double strikethrough	Outline	All caps
Superscript	Emboss	Hidden
Subscript	Engrave	

Insert Symbols

- Select the **Insert** tab and the **Symbol** command. Recently used symbols will be displayed in the drop down menu. Select **More Symbols**
- The **Symbol** dialog box will open. Click the **Font** drop down arrow and choose a symbol font, such as **Webdings** or **Wingdings**
- Click a symbol and then click **Insert**. Click **Close**

Insert Special Characters

- Select the **Insert** tab and the **Symbol** command. Recently used symbols will be displayed in the drop down menu. Select **More Symbols**
- The **Symbol** dialog box will open. Click the **Special Characters** tab.
- Click a character, such as © and then click **Insert**. Click **Close**

Change Case

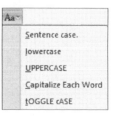

- Highlight the word and then select the **Change Case** button from the **Home** tab and the **Font** group. Select an option from the list
- The shortcut key combination to move between all of the change case options is *Shift* and *F3*.

 © Lorna Bointon, Qualiteach Education 2014

Copy Formatting

- Highlight the formatted text. Click once or double-click the **Format Painter** button from the **Home** tab/**Clipboard** group (by double clicking, the button remains active; click once and the button remains active for one action only)
- Highlight the text which is to display the same formatting

Applying Built-in Styles

- Highlight the text and then select the **More** button in the **Styles** group to see all available styles for the current document.

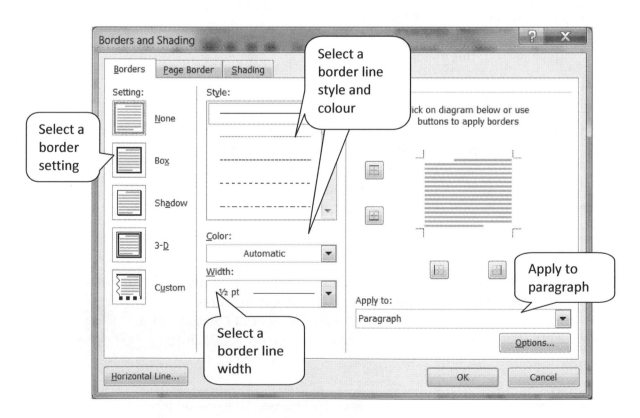

- The available styles for the current document will be displayed. Select a style.

Paragraph Borders

- Select the paragraph and then from the **Home** tab/**Paragraph** group, select the **Borders** button. Choose a border from the drop down menu or select **No Border** to remove a border
- To see further border and shading options, select **Borders and Shading**
- Choose options as shown below:

© Lorna Bointon, Qualiteach Education 2014

Paragraph Shading

- Select the **Borders** button and **Borders and Shading**, and then select the **Shading** tab to see the shading options.
- From the **Fill Color** drop down menu, select a colour, ensure that **Paragraph** is selected in the **Apply to** box and then click **OK**.

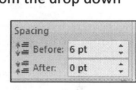

Layout Techniques

Note: for basic layout techniques such as margins, alignment and orientation etc, see the **Level 1** Functional Skills Activity Workbook and Revision Guide

Paragraph Spacing

- Select the text or position the cursor within a paragraph and then select the **Line Spacing** button from the **Home** tab and the **Paragraph** group. Select **Remove Space Before Paragraph** or **Add Space After Paragraph** from the drop down list

- For more paragraph spacing options, select the **Page Layout** tab and increase or decrease the **Spacing** measurement for **Before** or **After** in the **Paragraph** group

Indentation

- Select the **Decrease** or **Increase Indents** buttons in the Paragraph group or use the **Ruler Bar.** The top indent marker creates a first line indent and the bottom indent marker creates a hanging indent. If both top and bottom indent markers are lined up on the Ruler, this creates a full indentation at the specified position:

First line indent at 1cm   Hanging indent at 1cm

Full indent at 1cm

- Alternatively, select the **Paragraph** dialog box launcher and select an indentation from the **Paragraph** dialog box:

Select a left and/or right indent

Choose First Line or Hanging and select BY how much

Vertical Alignment

- Select the **Page Layout** tab and then click the **Page Setup** dialog box launcher icon
- Click the **Layout** tab and then select the **Vertical Alignment** arrow and choose an option (Top is the default setting)

   © Lorna Bointon, Qualiteach Education 2014

Page Border

- For a page border, select the **Page Borders** button from the **Page Layout** tab and **Page Background** group
- Select a setting, style, colour and width
- Select the **Art** drop down list to see a list of pictorial borders. Click OK

Headers and Footers

- **Microsoft® Word**: From the **Insert** tab, select **Header or Footer**

Choose Header or Footer

- Select the type of header or footer that you want from the menu or select **Edit Header/Footer** to make changes to an existing header or footer. The **Header & Footer Tools** ribbon becomes available
- Enter the required information in the header or footer area
- Select the **Close Header and Footer** button

Footer -Section 2-

59   Copyright © Qualiteach Education 2010

Footer

- **Microsoft® Excel:** From the **Insert** tab, select **Header & Footer.**
- The **Header & Footer Tools** ribbon becomes available. Enter the required information in the header or footer area
- **Microsoft® PowerPoint:** From the **Insert** tab, select **Header & Footer.**
- The **Header and Footer** dialog box appears. Enter text that is to appear in the footer in the **Footer** box, select **Date & Time** to include a date on the slides, select **Slide Number** to insert a number on each slide. Click **Apply to All** to apply the footer to all slides or Apply to add the footer to the currently selected slide.

Columns

- Select the **Columns** command from the **Page Layout** tab. Choose the desired amount of columns. Select **More Columns** to see further options, such as column width and spacing.

Page Numbers

- From the **Insert** tab and the **Header & Footer** group, select the **Page Number** button
- Select an option from the drop down list, e.g. Top of Page or Bottom of Page, and select an alignment from the submenu. The **Header & Footer Tools** ribbon becomes available. Select the **Close Header and Footer** button

Page Breaks

- To create a manual (hard) page break, position the cursor where the page break is to be inserted and then press the **Ctrl** key and the Enter key.
- Alternatively, select the **Page Layout** tab and then select the **Breaks** command. Select **Page** from the drop down list.
- Page breaks can be viewed on the page by selecting the **Show/Hide** button from the **Home** tab. ·················Page Break·················
- To delete a page break (only possible with a manually inserted page break and not a soft page break) click onto the page break and press **Delete**

Section Breaks

- To create a section break, select the **Page Layout** tab and then select the **Break**s command.
- In the **Section Breaks** section of the drop down menu, select an option
  - ○ a **Continuous Section Break** is needed if the heading is to span 2 or more columns
  - ○ A **Next Page** section break should be used to create a new section on a separate page.

Column Breaks

- Select the **Page Layout** tab and then select the **Break**s command. Click **Column** to create a column break.

Tabs

- Click the **Tab Style** button(left hand side of Ruler Bar as shown below) to select the desired tab style, e.g. left, right, centre, decimal (decimal tabs are used with prices etc to line up the decimal point)
- Click the Ruler Bar in the desired position to create a tab stop). The tabs are displayed on the Ruler Bar (see below).
- Press the **Tab** key to move the cursor to each tab stop position

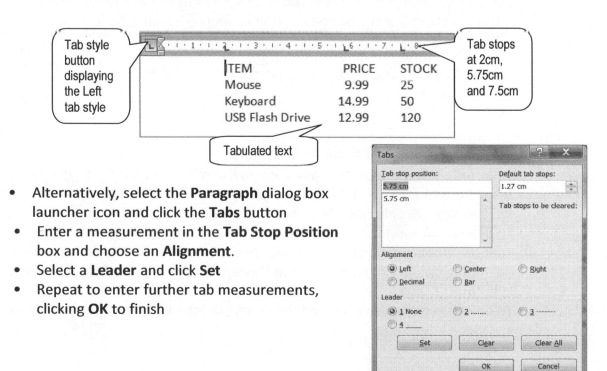

Tab style button displaying the Left tab style

ITEM	PRICE	STOCK
Mouse	9.99	25
Keyboard	14.99	50
USB Flash Drive	12.99	120

Tab stops at 2cm, 5.75cm and 7.5cm

Tabulated text

- Alternatively, select the **Paragraph** dialog box launcher icon and click the **Tabs** button
- Enter a measurement in the **Tab Stop Position** box and choose an **Alignment**.
- Select a **Leader** and click **Set**
- Repeat to enter further tab measurements, clicking **OK** to finish

 © Lorna Bointon, Qualiteach Education 2014

Tables

- From the **Insert** tab select **Table**
- Select **Insert Table** from the drop down list
- Choose the number of rows and columns that you need for the table and click **OK**

> Choose the amount of rows and columns required for the table

> Click **OK** to create the table

Merge Cells

- Select the columns to be merged and then from the **Table Tools/Layout** tab, select **Merge Cells**.

Split Cells

- Select the columns to be merged and then from the **Table Tools/Layout** tab, select **Split Cells**. Choose the amount of columns or rows and click OK.

Borders and shading

- Select the table or the row(s) or column(s) to be formatted and then select the **Shading** button from the **Table Tools/Design** tab to apply or remove colour. Alternatively, select the **Borders** button to apply or remove borders.

> Select the shading button

> Select a border style from the drop down list

> **Tip:** Gridlines are different to borders and do not appear on printouts of a table.

Add/Remove Rows & Columns

- To insert a row, position the cursor in a row in the table and then choose from one of the options in the **Table Tools/Layout** tab and **Rows & Columns** group (Insert Below, Insert Above).
- To delete a row, select it and then select **Delete** and then **Delete Rows**.
- To insert a column, position the cursor in a column in the table and then choose from one of the options in the **Table Tools/Layout** tab and **Rows & Columns** group (Insert Left, Insert Right).
- To delete a column, select it and then select **Delete** and then **Delete Columns**.

 © Lorna Bointon, Qualiteach Education 2014

Table Formulas

- Position the cursor in the cell where the formula is to appear and then, from the **Table Tools/Layout** tab, select **Formula**.
- The **Formula** dialog box opens. The default function is SUM. The formula will display (ABOVE) if cursor is positioned below the numerical range being calculated or (LEFT), depending on the current cursor position in the table.
- Choose a number format from the drop down list to display decimal places or currency.
- The Paste Function drop down list displays a list of different functions, such as Average and Count.
- Click OK.

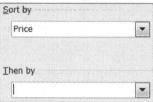

NOTE: the formula can be updated to reflect any changes made to the numerical data used in the calculation by selecting the formula and then pressing the **F9** key.

Sort data in a table

- Select the data in the table to be sorted, including the headings. From the **Table Tools/Layout** tab, select the **Sort** button. The **Sort** dialog box opens.
- Select the **Sort By** drop down arrow and choose a heading to sort by. Select the correct **Type** (e.g. **Number**). Select a sort order option button.
- Choose to sort on a second level by selecting a heading from the **Then By** drop down list.
- Ensure that the **My list Has header row** radio is selected.
- Click OK.

Table Tools/Layout tab

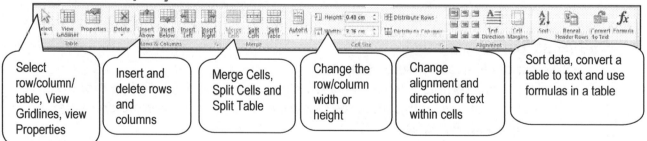

| Select row/column/ table, View Gridlines, view Properties | Insert and delete rows and columns | Merge Cells, Split Cells and Split Table | Change the row/column width or height | Change alignment and direction of text within cells | Sort data, convert a table to text and use formulas in a table |

 © Lorna Bointon, Qualiteach Education 2014

Templates

Create a new template

- Select the **File** tab and then select **New**
- The **Available Templates** window opens.
- Choose a template type and then click the **Template** radio button. Click **Create**. Alternatively, select a template category from Office.com Templates and click **Download**.
- A new document, based on the chosen template will be displayed on screen.

- Alternatively, create a new document. Enter information into the document as required and then save as a template (see below).

Save as Template:

- Select the **File** tab and then **Save As**.
- Select **Word Template** from the **Save as Type** drop down list. Ensure that the template will save with a .dotx file extension in the correct drive/folder, enter a filename and click **Save**.

NOTE: templates will automatically save in the **Templates** folder unless you choose a different folder/drive.

 © Lorna Bointon, Qualiteach Education 2014

Have a Go

Try the activities below to test yourself on the previous section

Match Makers

Match the correct answer to the questions below:

1.	Automatic page break generated by the software	a	Next Page
2.	This break should be used to ensure that a heading spans 2 or more columns	b	Continuous section
3.	This break should be used to create a new section on a separate page	c	Hard Page Break
4.	A manual page break entered by a user	d	Soft Page Break

Enter your answers below:

1.		2.		3.		4.	

As Easy As....

A B C

1. A type of font effect that displays characters above the normal line of text?

A	Subscript	☐
B	Sans Serif	☐
C	Serif	☐
D	Superscript	☐

2. Columns are a suitable layout technique to enhance the presentation of which of the following?

A	A folded leaflet	☐
B	A newsletter	☐
C	An advert	☐
D	All of the above	☐

Practice Makes Perfect

6.1a

Practical Exercise 1

1. Create a new document in Microsoft® Word and save it as a template called **Newsletter**

2. Change the orientation to landscape

3. Change the left and right margins to 3cm

4. Insert two columns

5. Add a page number to the footer and your name to the header

6. Re-save the template

Practical Exercise 2

1. Enter the heading **My Hobbies** and make sure that it spans both columns

2. Format the heading with appropriate fonts and sizes

3. Enter a list of your hobbies/interests.

4. Use bullets and line spacing to enhance the list of hobbies

5. Using appropriate fonts and sizes provide more information on each of your hobbies and interests under relevant subheadings.

6. Use images from photos or Clipart and shapes to enhance the newsletter. See the example below.

7. Save as a document called **hobbies** and close

Candidate Name

MY HOBBIES

- Walking
- Reading
- Crosswords
- Wildlife

WALKING
I love walking in the Welsh hills, especially around Moel Famau and Cilcain.

Another favourite walking area is Bickerton and Peckforton in Cheshire, although these do not afford hill climbs as steep as Moel Famau.

READING
My favourite books are historical detective novels or whodunits.

I also like reading books on wildlife and natural medicine.

Crosswords
I prefer cryptic crosswords, particularly the Times crossword, although I do find this hard!

Wildlife
I like to identify wild flowers when on a walk and use a reference guide to find any that I can't identify.

I also like to watch and identify birds and memorise all of the Latin names.

1

 © Lorna Bointon, Qualiteach Education 2014

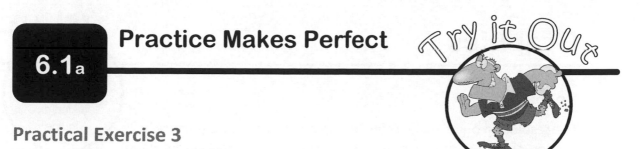

Practical Exercise 3

1.   Create a new document.

2.   Create a table as shown below (using borders, shading and merged cells):

INVOICE			
Product Code	**Quantity**	**Price**	**Total**
		Subtotal	
		P&P	
		Total	

3.   Save the document as a template called **Temp_invoice** and close.

Practical Exercise 4

1.   Open **Temp_invoice** and save as a document called **Invoice_1**.

2.   Enter the data as shown below:

Product Code	Quantity	Price	Total
A01	4	10.00	40.00
A02	1	15.00	15.00

3.   Enter a formula for the **Subtotal** that will calculate the sum total of all three products.

4.   Enter **4.50** as the **P&P**. Enter a formula in the **Total** cell that will add the post and packaging to the subtotal to find the final total. Save **Invoice_1** and close.

Graphics

Did You Know?

Reducing the amount of pixels can distort an image

Resolution

The resolution of an image refers to the amount of pixels (picture elements) or tiny squares that make up the picture. More pixels mean better quality but also higher file sizes. Resolution of a printed image needs to be higher than an image which will be viewed on-screen, such as on a web page.

The examples below show two copies of the same digital photo, the first has high resolution and the second has reduced resolution resulting in a 'pixelated' image.

Graphics can be resized and cropped to make them suitable for inclusion in documents. Image size can be increased or reduced by resizing and parts of an image can be removed by using the cropping tool. Images can be positioned accurately on a page by using the Picture tools.

Uncropped image

Image cropped to show only the cow in the forefront

When an image is selected it is surrounded by small blobs – these are resizing handles. When the mouse arrow is placed over a resizing handle, the mouse pointer turns into a double headed black arrow. Drag the mouse inwards and/or downwards to reduce the size or drag outwards and upwards to increase the size. To ensure that images maintain the original proportions without distortion, the Lock Aspect Ratio option should be selected before resizing the height OR the width. Always resize manually via a corner resizing handle.

Insert Clip Art

- Position the cursor where the image is to be inserted. Select the **Insert** tab
- Select the **Clip Art** button and the Clip Art task pane will open
- Type an image name/description into the **Search for** box (e.g. computer) and press the **Go** button
- The Clip Art gallery will display images matching the search words that you entered. Select an image to insert it into the document or slide.

Insert an image from file

- Position the cursor in the document or slide where the image is to be inserted. Select the **Insert** tab
- Select the **Picture** button and the **Insert Picture** dialog box will appear
- Find and select the required image file and then click **Insert**

Crop or resize a picture

Picture Tools/Format tab

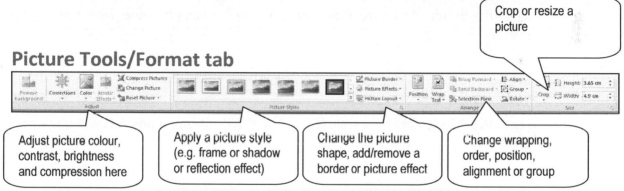

Adjust picture colour, contrast, brightness and compression here

Apply a picture style (e.g. frame or shadow or reflection effect)

Change the picture shape, add/remove a border or picture effect

Change wrapping, order, position, alignment or group

Resize an image

- Click the image and resizing handles will appear around the image
- Move the mouse pointer over a corner resizing handle (always drag from a corner handle to maintain image proportions) and drag inwards and downwards to reduce the size or outwards and upwards to increase the size
- Images can also be resized accurately by selecting **Shape Height** or **Shape Width** measurements from the **Picture Tools/Layout** tab and the **Size** group. Choose whether to change the height or width measurement

Crop an image

- Select the image and then select the **Crop** tool from the **Picture Tools/Format** tab

- Move the mouse pointer over one of the crop handles and drag to crop parts of the image

Wrap an image

- Click on the image and then select the **Wrap Text** command from the **Picture Tools/Format** tab

- Select a wrapping style from the drop down list:

  In Line with Text – this is the default wrapping style for inserted images. The image will be positioned on the same line as text.
  Square –wraps text squarely around the image
  Tight –wraps text tightly around the image
  Behind Text – image will be positioned behind text
  In Front of Text – image will be positioned in front of text enabling free movement of the image on the page

Align an image

The **In Line With Text** wrapping style should be applied to a selected image before being aligned using the Alignment tools.

- Select the image. From the **Home** tab and the **Paragraph** group, select an Alignment button.

Position an image

If the **In Line With Text** wrapping style is applied, the Position commands will not work so choose a different wrapping style.

- Select the image and then select the **Picture Tools/Format** tab
- Select the **Position** button
- Select **More Layout Options** from the menu
- Select the **Picture Position** tab and make changes to the current **Horizontal** and/or **Vertical** position of the image
- Click **OK**

Move an Image

- Position mouse pointer over image, hold down mouse button (black cross icon appears) and drag (will not work if In Line with Text wrapping style applied).

Reduce Image Resolution

- Select the image and then select the **Picture Tools/Format** tab.

- Select the **Compress Pictures** command from the **Adjust** group. Tick the **Apply only to this picture** checkbox. Choose options from the **Target output** section, (subject to how the image will be viewed), such as **Screen (150 ppi) good for web pages and projectors**. Click **OK**.

 © Lorna Bointon, Qualiteach Education 2014

Match Makers

Match the correct answer to the questions below:

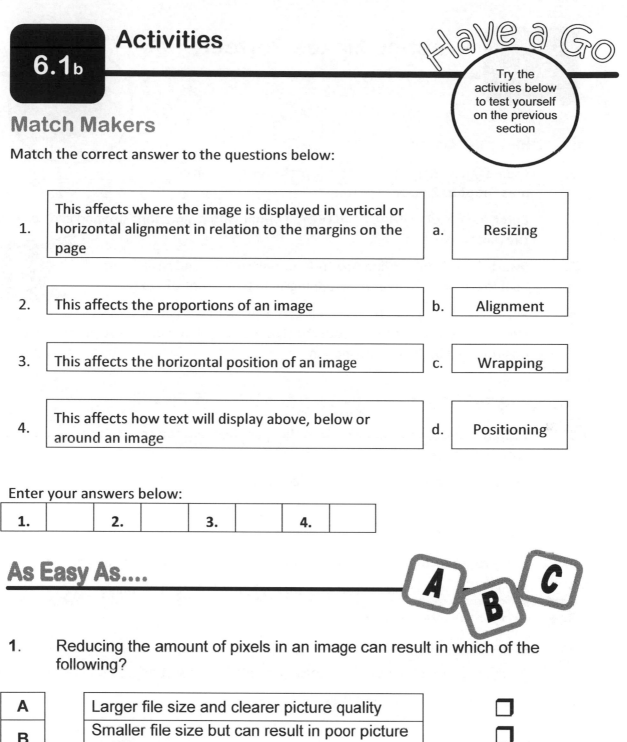

1.	This affects where the image is displayed in vertical or horizontal alignment in relation to the margins on the page	a. Resizing
2.	This affects the proportions of an image	b. Alignment
3.	This affects the horizontal position of an image	c. Wrapping
4.	This affects how text will display above, below or around an image	d. Positioning

Enter your answers below:

1.		2.		3.		4.	

As Easy As.... A B C

1. Reducing the amount of pixels in an image can result in which of the following?

A	Larger file size and clearer picture quality	☐
B	Smaller file size but can result in poor picture quality	☐
C	Smaller file size and clearer picture quality	☐
D	It has no effect on file size or picture quality	☐

2. The decision to modify picture resolution depends on which of the following?

A	Whether it is to be viewed on-screen	☐
B	Whether it will be sent as an attachment via email	☐
C	Whether it will be printed as hard-copy output	☐
D	All of the above	☐

Practical Exercise 1

1.   Create a new document in Microsoft® Word and save it as **GraphicL2.docx**

2.   Enter the heading **IMAGE GALLERY**. Format with a large font size and centre across the page

3.   Insert the following Clipart picture (or one similar) and resize it to 3cm in height. Change the wrapping style to **In Front of Text**.

4.   Position the image so that it is has **Left** alignment with an absolute Horizontal position of 6cm from the right of the column and an absolute Vertical position of 8cm below the margin.

Practical Exercise 2

1.   Crop the image to remove most of the grass beneath the cow, but be careful not to crop the hooves.

2.   Resize the image so that it is now 5cm in height

Practical Exercise 3

1.   Compress the image to 96ppi, making it suitable for sending via email.

2.   Apply the Reflected Rounded Rectangle Picture Style to the image.

3.   Recolor the image in Grayscale.

4.   Apply a grey border to the image.

5.   Apply a picture effect of your choice (e.g. shadow or soft edges etc).

6.   Resave the document and close.

Example

Drawing Tools

Did You Know?

Drawing tools can be used to create multi-layered images

Drawing tools are used to create shapes, such as circles, ovals, squares, text boxes, arrows etc. These can be used in conjunction with images and WordArt to create a complex multi-layered picture.

See the examples below:

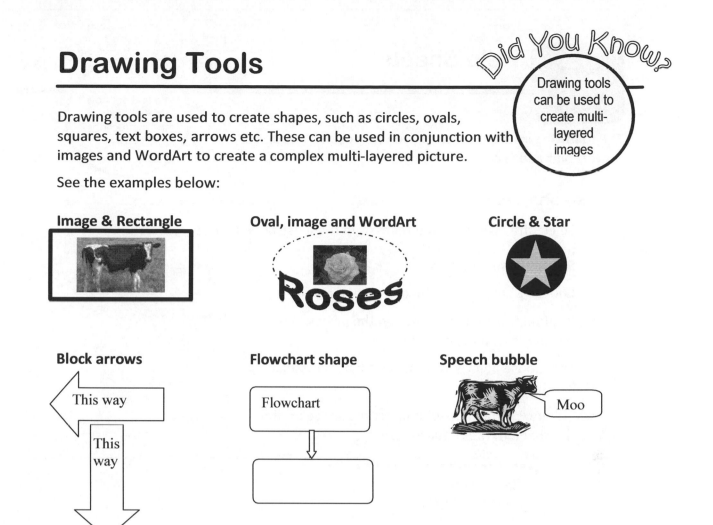

Image & Rectangle

Oval, image and WordArt

Circle & Star

Block arrows

This way

This way

Flowchart shape

Flowchart

Speech bubble

Moo

Shapes can be formatted with colour, lines and text and can be structured to appear in a different order (i.e. Bring to front, Send to back etc) and then grouped together to make one object. The example below uses images, text and shapes to create a mind map for Evaluation.

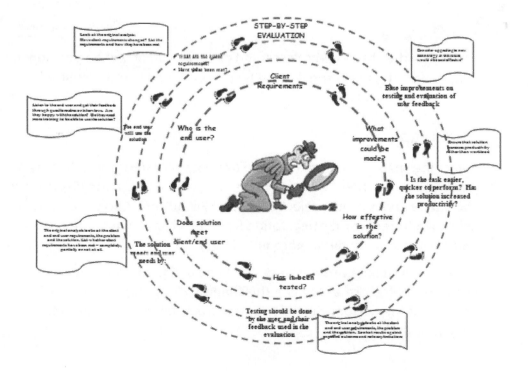

The following instructions work with Microsoft® Word, PowerPoint and Excel.

Create Shapes

- Select the **Insert** tab and then, from the **Illustrations** group, select the **Shapes** command.

- Choose a shape from the drop-down menu.

- Position the mouse pointer on the page where the shape is to be inserted.

- The mouse pointer displays as a black crosshair icon

- Either click the mouse to insert the shape or drag the shape to the required size

> **Tip**: Hold down the **Shift** key when dragging a rectangle or oval shape to create a perfect square or circle

Recently Used Shapes

Lines

Basic Shapes

Block Arrows

Flowchart

Callouts

Stars and Banners

New Drawing Canvas

Insert Text

- Right click the shape and select **Add Text**. The cursor will be positioned within the shape. Start typing in the desired text. Format the text as required.

Format a shape

- Select the shape and then, from the **Drawing Tools/Format** tab (may be displayed as the **Text Box Tools** depending on type of shape inserted) and the **Shape Styles** group, select the **Shape Fill** button. Choose a colour or select a different formatting option from the drop-down menu (gradient, texture, picture, pattern, no fill or more fill colours)

- To format a shape border, select the shape and then, from the **Drawing Tools/Format** tab and the **Shape Styles** group, select the **Shape Outline** button. Select an option from the menu (such as Outline colour, weight or dash style)

Select Shapes

- Click an individual shape to select it.
- Hold down the **CTRL** key and click each shape to select multiple shapes

Order Shapes

- Select a shape and then, from the **Drawing Tools/Format** tab (may be displayed as the **Text Box Tools** depending on type of shape inserted) and the **Arrange** group, select the **Bring Forward** or **Send Backward** buttons and choose an option from the drop-down menu.

Group shapes

- Select each of the shapes and then right click and select **Grouping** and then **Group**

Ungrouped Images

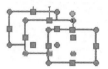

Grouped images

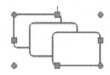

Rotate shapes

- Select the shape and then drag the rotation handle in the desired direction:

- Alternatively, select the **Rotate** button on the **Drawing Tools/Format** ribbon and select an option from the menu (e.g. Flip Horizontal/Vertical or Rotate Right 90^{0}etc)

Drawing Tools Ribbon:

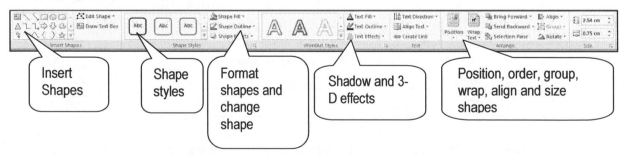

© Lorna Bointon, Qualiteach Education 2014

Match Makers

Match the correct answer to the questions by identifying the correct types of shape below:

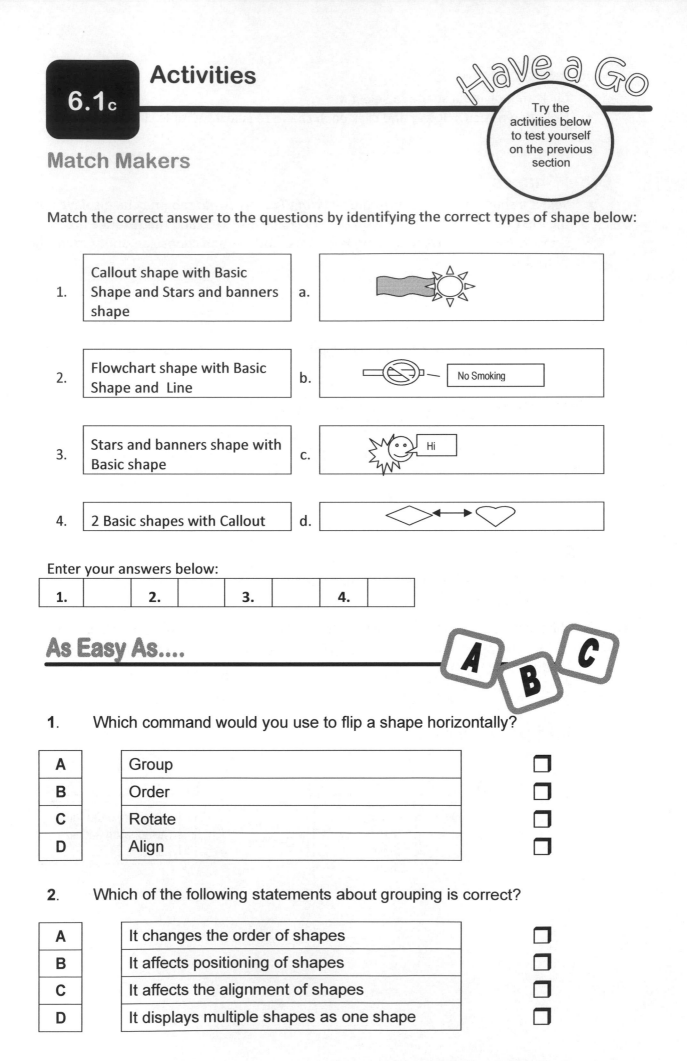

1.	Callout shape with Basic Shape and Stars and banners shape	a.
2.	Flowchart shape with Basic Shape and Line	b.
3.	Stars and banners shape with Basic shape	c.
4.	2 Basic shapes with Callout	d.

Enter your answers below:

1.		2.		3.		4.	

As Easy As....

A B C

1. Which command would you use to flip a shape horizontally?

A	Group	☐
B	Order	☐
C	Rotate	☐
D	Align	☐

2. Which of the following statements about grouping is correct?

A	It changes the order of shapes	☐
B	It affects positioning of shapes	☐
C	It affects the alignment of shapes	☐
D	It displays multiple shapes as one shape	☐

Practical Exercise 1

1. Create a new document in Microsoft® Word and save it as **ShapeL2.docx**

2. Insert a Punched Tape flowchart shape

3. Format the shape with a yellow fill colour and thick brown dashed line style

4. Resize the shape to be 3cm height and 5cm width

5. Add the following text to the shape **Go with...**

6. Format the text with different font, size, style and colour

Practical Exercise 2

1. Insert a right pointing block arrow and position it like the one shown below:

2. Make a copy of the flowchart shape and position it at the tip of the arrow.

3. Change the text to **....with the flow!**

Practical Exercise 3

1. Group the shapes together to make one shape

2. Align the shape horizontally in the middle of the page

3. Add a text box above the shape and enter the text **Take it easy...**

4. Remove the border and any fill colour

5. Format the text to make it stand out

6. Insert the smiley face shape in front of the text and format with a colour fill

7. Copy the shape to the end of the text

8. Rotate the copied shape so that it is about 45^0 clockwise

9. Rotate the first smiley face so it is about 45^0 anti-clockwise. Save and close.

Example

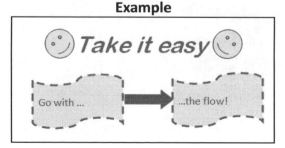

Presentations

Note: for more information on presentations see the **Level 1** Functional Skills Activity Workbook and Revision Guide

Did You Know?

A master slide is the formatted template on which all slides are based

Master Slide

To ensure consistency throughout a presentation, the formatting, such as fonts, font sizes, font colours, font styles, background colour and logos and any other standard content (i.e. any content which will appear on every slide in the presentation) is applied to a master slide which is a type of template on which slides within the presentation are based.

A professional slide show contains opening and closing slides and consistent formatting through the presentation.

Transitions and Animations

The way that each slide is presented on screen is controlled by applying a transition between each slide. Slide content can be animated on each slide.

Printing

Slides can be printed as handouts (miniature or thumbnail) on a page and also as audience handouts with 3 slides per page and space for notes at the side of each slide.

PowerPoint Shows

Slides which are saved as PowerPoint Shows can be run on a computer that does not have PowerPoint software installed.

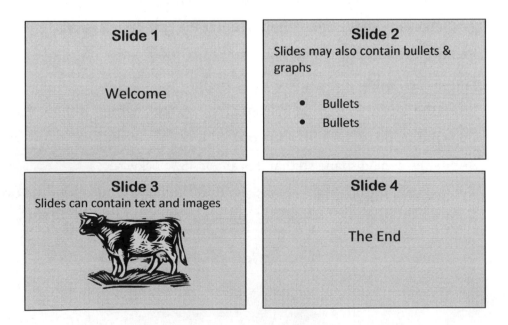

Help Sheets

6.1d

To find out how to do it, follow the instructions below

Create a Master Slide

- Select the **Slide Master** button from the **View** tab and the **Presentation Views** group
- Format the slide areas as desired (select formatting tools from the **Home** tab)

Apply Background Colour

- Ensure that Master Slide view is selected. Select the **Background Styles** button. Select **Format Background**. Make sure that the **Solid Fill** option button is selected. Select the **Color** arrow and choose a colour. Click **Apply to All**. Click **Close**.

Insert New Slide

- Ensure that Normal view is selected and then select the **New Slide** button from the **Home** tab. Select a slide layout.

Change the slide layout

Insert a new slide

Change Slide Layout

- In Normal view, select the **Layout** button from the **Home** tab. Select a slide layout.

Diagrams and Flowcharts

- In Normal view, select the **Smart Art** button from the **Insert** tab. Select a diagram or flowchart shape and click **OK**.

Slide Footers

- From the **Insert** tab, select **Headers & Footer**.
- Click the **Date and time** tick box to add the date; ensure that it will update automatically with a new date by clicking the **Update automatically** radio button
- Ensure that the language is **English (UK)**
- Select the **Slide Number** tick box to insert a slide number and click the **Footer** tick box and then enter the footer text. De-select **Don't show on title slide** if you want *all* slide layouts to display footer
- Click **Apply** to apply to the current slide or **Apply to All** to apply to all slides in the presentation.

Print

- From the **File** tab select **Print**.
- To print each slide, ensure that **Print All Slides** and **Full Page Slides** are both selected in the **Settings** section and then select the **Print** button.

Print handouts

- From the **Print** window, select the **Settings** arrow beside **Full Page Slides** and then, in the **Handouts** section of the menu, select the amount of slides to appear on each page (choose whether to display the slides in vertical or horizontal order). Click **Print**.

Audience Handouts 3 per page   **Handouts 6 slides horizontal**

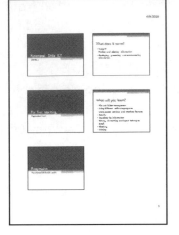

Insert Objects (graphs/tables)

- From the **Home** tab, select the **Title and Content** slide layout
- To insert a chart, click the **Insert Chart** icon. Choose a chart type and click **OK**. Enter data into the spreadsheet to create the chart and then close the spreadsheet on completion. The **Chart Tools** tab becomes available when the chart is selected.
- To insert a table, select the **Insert Table** icon. Choose the required amount of table rows/columns and click **OK**. The **Table Tools** tab becomes active when the table is selected.

Select an icon, such as Table or Chart

Movies, SmartArt and images can also be inserted

Insert Movie Clips & Sound Files

Movie clips:

- Select the **Insert** tab and then, from the **Media** group, click **Video**.

- Select Video from File.

- Locate the video file and click **OK**.

- Videos can also be inserted from the Clip Art Video gallery. Select this option from the Video menu, and then choose a movie/video clip from the task pane.
- The Video Tools/Format and Playback tabs become available when the video clip is selected. Select Playback to choose how it will start (on click or automatically)

Sound files

- Select the **Insert** tab and then, from the **Media** group, click **Audio**.

- Select **Audio from File** if it is saved on your computer, or select from **Clip Art Audio** option to insert a sound from the Clipart gallery.

- Locate the sound file and click **OK**.
- The Audio Tools/Format and Playback tabs become available when the audio clip is selected. Select Playback to choose how it will start (on click or automatically)

Apply Transitions

- In Slide Sorter view, select the **Transitions** tab
- From the **Transition to This Slide** group, select the **More** button

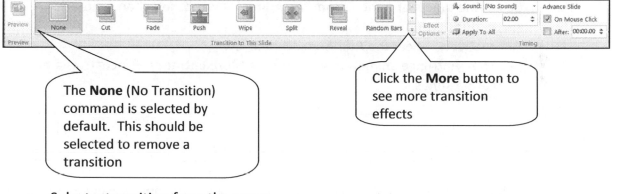

The **None** (No Transition) command is selected by default. This should be selected to remove a transition

Click the **More** button to see more transition effects

- Select a transition from the menu
- Move the mouse over a transition to see a tag displaying the effect's name
- Click a transition to select it
- The transition will be applied to the currently selected slide

A transition effect is indicated by the following symbol beneath a slide

- Double click this symbol to see a preview of the transition effect
- Select the duration of the transition from the Timing group
- To apply the selected transition to all slides in the presentation, click the **Apply to All** command

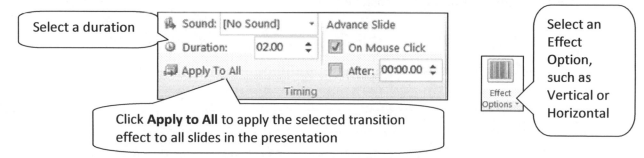

Select a duration

Select an Effect Option, such as Vertical or Horizontal

Click **Apply to All** to apply the selected transition effect to all slides in the presentation

 © Lorna Bointon, Qualiteach Education 2014

Apply Timings

- Automatic transition timings can be set by selecting a time in the **After** box (or choose to control the slide show by **On Mouse Click**)

- To apply the selected transition to all slides in the presentation, click the **Apply to All** command

Loop Continuously

- Select the **Slide Show** tab and then the **Set Up Slide Show** button.
- The **Set Up Show** window will appear.
- Ensure that the **Loop continuously until 'Esc'** box is *checked*:
- Click OK.

Apply Animations

- Select the object and then, from the **Animations** tab, select an **Animation** from the Animations group**.**
- Alternatively, select the **Add Animation** arrow.
- Select an entrance animation style or click **More Entrance Effects** to see more animation styles.

- Select the **Animation Pane** command to view a list of animations applied to objects on the slide.
- Select options from the **Timing** group to start the animation and control the duration.
- Select the **Effect Options** arrow to change animation effect settings.
- Click the **Preview** button to see the animation effects.

Save as a PowerPoint Show

- Select the **File** tab and **Save As**. Ensure that the correct drive/folder is selected from the **Save in** drop down list.
- From the **Save as Type** drop down arrow, select **PowerPoint Show (*.ppsx)**
- Enter a filename and click **Save**

 © Lorna Bointon, Qualiteach Education 2014

Match Makers

Match the correct answer to the questions below:

1.	A professional presentation will start and finish with these...	a.	Audience handouts
2.	This type of printout enables viewers to add notes against thumbnail slides	b.	Transition
3.	This effect can be applied to slide content	c.	Opening and closing slides
4.	This effect changes the way that each slide appears	d.	Animation

Enter your answers below:

1.		2.		3.		4.	

As Easy As....

A B C

1. A slide show can be saved in this format to enable it to be run on a computer without PowerPoint software?

A	PowerPoint Template	☐
B	PowerPoint Macro Enabled	☐
C	PowerPoint Show	☐
D	PowerPoint Presentation	☐

2. This ensures consistency throughout the presentation as it contains formatting that will be used on each of the slides that are based on it?

A	Master Slide	☐
B	Master Template	☐
C	Template Slide	☐
D	Title Slide	☐

Practical Exercise 1

1.	Create a new presentation in Microsoft® PowerPoint and save it as **Marine.pptx**

2.	Using the master slide, format the background with a colour of your choice. Format the heading, subheading and bullet text with fonts, sizes and colour of your choice.

3.	Insert a suitable image for the subject (marine life) and ensure that it is resized and positioned appropriately on the Master Slide

4.	Create a Title Only slide with the heading **Marine Life in West Wales**

5.	Insert a new slide to hold a title and bulleted text. Enter the heading: **Marine Sightings.** Enter the following bulleted text:

- Dolphins
- Porpoises
- Whales
- Seals

6.	Insert a new slide to hold a title and bulleted text. Enter the heading: **Locations in West Wales.** Enter the following bulleted text:

- Cardigan Bay
- Pembrokeshire
- Cardiff Bay
- Fishguard

7.	Insert a sound clip of ocean waves from the ClipArt gallery. Ensure that it will start When Clicked.

8.	Insert a new Title and Content slide and insert a pie chart with the following data:

	Sightings
Dolphins	20
Porpoises	15
Whales	10
Seals	45

Practical Exercise 2

1.	Apply a transition of your choice between each slide

2.	Apply a duration of 5 seconds between each slide

3.	Apply a **Fly In By Category** animated effect to the pie chart

4.	Add a blank closing slide with the text **The End, Thank you for watching** and re-save

5.	Re-save the presentation as a PowerPoint Show.

6.	Print the presentation as a handout with 5 slides per page. Close the presentation and exit PowerPoint

Section 7 ▶

Developing, Presenting and Communicating
Information

Data

Use appropriate software to meet requirements of a complex data-handling task

Numerical Data

Did You Know?

The BODMAS method ensures a correct result

Note: for basic information on spreadsheets see the **Level 1** Functional Skills Activity Workbook and Revision Guide

Arithmetic Formulas

Every formula starts with the equals sign = and uses arithmetic operators for addition, subtraction, division and multiplication:

+   Addition

-       Subtraction

/   Division

*   Multiplication

Formulas should use cell references instead of numbers, such as A1, B2 etc, so that the formula will recalculate when the numbers change. For example:

	A	B	C
1	Price	Qty	Total
2	100.00	5	=100*5

The result will be **500.**
If numbers, such as the Qty, changes the formula will not recalculate

	A	B	C
1	Price	Qty	Total
2	100.00	5	=A2*B2

The result will still be **500.**
If numbers, such as the Qty, changes the formula will recalculate to reflect the change

BODMAS

Brackets are used in formulas to separate one part of the formula from another. The BODMAS principle determines where brackets should go. See the example below:

(B)rackets
(O)rder
(D)ivision
(M)ultiplication
(A)ddition
(S)ubtraction

$$=(A2-B2)*2$$

This means that, within a formula, numbers will divide before being multiplied, added or subtracted. In the following formula, the numbers will be multiplied first before being subtracted because there are no brackets.

See the examples overleaf:

BODMAS EXAMPLES

Without brackets
=10-5*2 result **0** (the formula is worked out as 5 multiplied by 2 then minus 10 =0)

With brackets
=(10-5)*2 result**10** (The formula is worked out by subtracting 5 from 10 then multiplying this result by 2)

Functions

Multiple cells may be used in a spreadsheet calculation, either separated by a comma, e.g. =SUM(A1,B1, C1) or by a colon to separate a cell range, e.g. =SUM(A1:C1).

Functions are used to find results, such as: the sum total, average, minimum or maximum figures in a spreadsheet.   Other functions include:

- **SUM** – finds the total of a range of cells
- **Count** – this counts the number of cells containing numbers or values within a list
- **Average** – this finds an average number within a range of numbers
- **Maximum**– this finds the largest number within a range of numbers
- **Minimum**– this finds the smallest number within a range of numbers
- **IF** – a logical argument that checks if a condition is met and returns one value if TRUE and another if FALSE.
- **VLOOKUP** – looks for a value in the leftmost column of a table and then returns a value in the same row from a column you specify. The table must be sorted in ascending order
- **HLOOKUP** – looks for a value in the top row of a table or array of values and returns the value in the same column from a row you specify

Referencing

Using *relative* cell references used within a formula or function, such as A1 or B1, ensures that it will recalculate to reflect changes made to the data used in the calculation. It also ensures that a formula can be replicated (copied) to other cells in the spreadsheet and the cell references in the formula will change for each row that is affected. If you don't want cell references to change when you copy a formula, for example if a cell should remain constant such as VAT 17.5%, then you should use *absolute cell references.* An absolute cell reference is shown below:

=B12*A1 refers to the contents of cell B12 being multiplied by the contents of cell A1(which is an absolute reference). When this formula is copied downwards to find the results for subsequent rows, the cell reference B12 will change to B13 because it is a *relative reference,* but the cell A1 will remain constant because it is ***Absolute***.

Formatting & Layout

A spreadsheet can be formatted to display gridlines and row and column headings to make it easier to read and locate data; headers and footers are applied to display page numbering, filename and location, author name, date and other information. Gridlines are displayed on screen to make it easier to use the spreadsheet and place data, but they are not displayed on a printout unless specified. To ensure that the spreadsheet data can be easily read when printed the setting to fit to one page can be used in conjunction with the orientation commands.

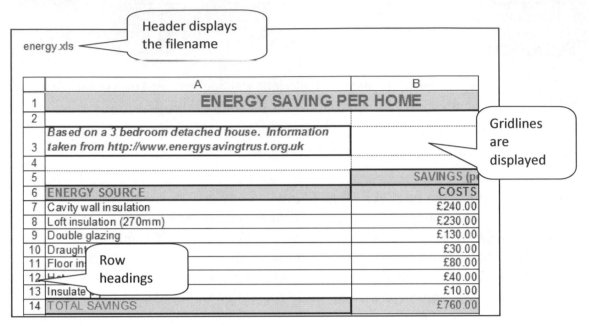

Replace Facility

To manually replace data within a large spreadsheet would be tedious and time consuming and could result in errors. Using the Replace facility in Microsoft Excel® is far more time efficient by enabling replacement of one or more items of data with replacement data in one action. The Replace facility allows the user to search for specified cell contents, either whole or partial, and then replace it with different data. The Replace facility will also replace part of a formula, for example: formulas containing the function SUM can be replaced by formulas containing the function AVERAGE. The Replace facility can also find cells with a specified format and replace them with a new format.

Importing text

Importing enables a user to import external data into a spreadsheet without creating a link to the source file. This is a useful way to use data that is contained in a text file, such as Note Pad or Word, within a spreadsheet. The file types *.csv* and *.txt* are known as generic file types because they are not application specific and can be used to transfer data from one application to another. A text file saved with a .csv file type will use commas to separate text items. Delimited refers to text files where each item of text is separated by tabs.

> **NOTE:** for basic spreadsheet formatting and layout instructions, such as data types, centre across columns and formatting and orientation etc see Functional Skills Activity Workbook and Revision Guide **Level 1**

Create a Formula

- Enter the **Equals** sign (=) followed by the first cell reference. Enter the arithmetic operator, such as +, -, /, * followed by the second cell reference (e.g. =A1*B1)

Show Formulas

- From the **Formulas** tab and the **Formulas Auditing** group, select the **Show Formulas** command.
- Alternatively, hold down the **Ctrl** key on the keyboard and press the **Grave accent** key (top left of the keyboard before the number 1 key). This is a *toggle* key which means that it is turned on/off each time it is pressed (e.g. when the key combination is pressed a second time, the formulas will be replaced by the values).

Use a Basic Function

- Click into the cell in which the result will be displayed. Select the **AutoSum** button (**Home** tab and **Editing** group). The SUM formula (e.g. =SUM(A1:C10) will display on the spreadsheet; click the **AutoSum** button again to complete the function.

- You can also enter a SUM function manually: type the equals sign (=), followed by the function name SUM. Type an open round bracket and then type the cell range separated by a colon (:). Close the bracket, e.g. =SUM(A1:C10).

Logical Functions

- Enter =IF(
- Enter the first condition e.g. =IF(B1>200

Comparison operators **(>) greater than, (<) less than, (=) equal to, (>=) greater than and equal to, (<=) less than and equal to**

- Enter a comma e.g. =IF(B1>200,
- Enter the result based on the condition being met (text must appear within quotes) e.g. =IF(B1>200, "YES"
- Enter a comma. Enter the result based on the condition **not** being met and close the bracket, e.g.=IF(B1>200, "YES", "NO")

If the contents of B1 are greater than 200 then YES will be returned, otherwise the result will be NO

Naming Cells

- Highlight the cell or cell range to be named.
- Click the cursor into the **Name** box and enter the name (spaces are disallowed; use the underscore _ in place of a space to separate names).
- Press the **Enter** key.

Lookup Functions

This function looks up a value in a range of cells (called an array). A Vlookup looks for values in the first *column* of a table and a Hlookup looks for values in the first *row* of a table.

- Click into the cell that is to display the results of the formula
- Select the **Formulas** tab
- From the **Function Library** group, select the **Lookup & Reference** arrow.
- Select **VLOOKUP** or **HLOOKUP** depending on the table array
- The Function Arguments window opens
- Enter the **Lookup_value** (or click the **Collapse Dialog** button at the end of the **Lookup_value** box and highlight the cell containing the lookup value. Click the **Restore Dialog** button to return to the function arguments box)
- Enter the table array name or cell range
- Enter the column or row in which the value is located. Click OK.

Insert & Delete Rows/Columns

- To delete rows or columns, select the row/column and then, from the **Home** tab and **Cells** group, select the **Delete** arrow. Choose **Delete Sheet Rows** or **Delete Sheet Columns**.
- To insert rows/columns select the row/column and then, from the **Home** tab and **Cells** group, select the **Insert** arrow. Choose **Insert Sheet Rows** or **Insert Sheet Columns**.

Replace

- Select the **Find & Select** command from the **Home** tab and choose **Replace** from the drop down menu
- The **Find and Replace** dialog box opens.
- Enter the **Find** data into the **Find what** box and the **Replacement** data in the **Replace with** box.
- Select **Replace All** to replace all occurrences of the search criteria
- Click the **Options >>** button to see further options:
  - Choose whether to search within the current sheet or the whole workbook
  - Choose whether to search by rows or by columns
  - Look in formulas
  - Find entire or partial cell contents
  - Match case (e.g. find cell contents that are in the same case as the search criteria)

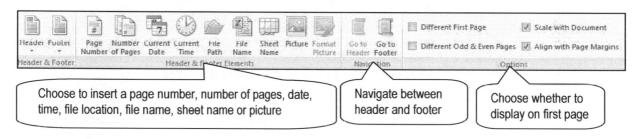

To search for cell contents based on format, click the **Format** arrow and select an existing format from the spreadsheet data or click the button to choose a format; click the **Replace with: Format** arrow and choose an existing replacement format from spreadsheet data or click the Format button to choose a format

Headers and Footers

- **Microsoft® Excel:** From the **Insert** tab, select **Header & Footer.**
- The **Header & Footer Tools** ribbon becomes available. Enter the required information in the header or footer area or select an option from the **Header & Footer Tools/Design** tab:

Choose to insert a page number, number of pages, date, time, file location, file name, sheet name or picture

Navigate between header and footer

Choose whether to display on first page

Import Text

- Open the spreadsheet into which the text file is to be imported.
- From the **Data** tab and the **Get External Data** group, select the **From Text** command.
- The **Import Text** File window opens. Select the correct drive/folder location from the Address bar drop-down menu. Ensure that **Text Files (*.prn; *.txt; *.csv)** is displayed in the **Files of type** box. Select the text file and click **Import**.
- The Import Text Wizard will begin. Ensure that the **Delimited** option button is selected.
- Click **Next >**
- At **Step 2 of 3**, ensure that the **Tab** delimiter tick box is selected.
- Ensure that " is displayed in the **Text Qualifier** box.
- Click **Next >**
- At **Step 3 of 3**, ensure that the **General** option button is selected.
- Click **Finish**
- The **Import Data** window will open. Choose one of the following option buttons:
- **Existing worksheet:** to import the data to the currently open spreadsheet, check that the correct cell reference is displayed and click OK.
- **New worksheet:** the data will be imported to a new worksheet within the open workbook. Click OK.
- Save the spreadsheet file.

Page Layout

- Commands such as Margins, Orientation (Portrait/Landscape) can be selected from the **Page Layout** tab and the **Page Setup** group.
- To display gridlines and/or row and column headings, select the **Print Titles** command from the **Page Layout** tab or click the dialog box launcher icon to open the **Page Setup** dialog box.
- Select the **Sheet** tab and select the tick boxes for **Gridlines** and **Row and Column Headings**
- Click OK.

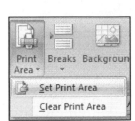

Fit to one page

- Select the **Page Layout** tab. Select the **Page Setup** dialog box launcher icon and the **Page** tab
- Click on the **Fit to:** radio button in the Scaling section. Ensure that 1 is selected and click on OK. (It will adjust the scaling of the page to a reduced percentage of the normal size).
- Click OK

Print Selection

- Highlight the cell range to be printed.
- Select the **Page Layout** tab and then, from the **Page Setup** group, select the **Print Area** command. Select **Set Print Area.**
- Select the **File** tab and then click **Print** and then click the **Print** button.
- De-select the print area by selecting **Print Area** and then **Clear Print Area**

Alternatively, print a selected cell range by selecting **File** tab and then **Print** and then, from the **Settings** drop down list (will currently display **Print Active Sheets**), select the **Print Selection** option. Click **Print**

Match Makers

Match the correct answer to the questions below:

1.	This function uses arguments and conditions		a	Absolute
2.	This function finds data by searching for a value in a specified row		b	IF
3.	This function finds data by searching for a value in a specified column		c	HLookup
4.	This cell reference remains constant		d	VLookup

Enter your answers below:

1.		2.		3.		4.	

As Easy As....

A B C

1.   These are used in formulas to ensure that the calculation is performed in the right order?

A	Quotation marks	☐
B	Brackets	☐
C	Colon	☐
D	Commas	☐

2.   In text file imports, delimited refers to which of the following?

A	Text separated by commas	☐
B	Un-separated text	☐
C	Text separated by tabs	☐
D	Text separated by spaces	☐

Practical Exercise 1

1. Create a new spreadsheet and save it as **Functions**

2. Enter the data below into the spreadsheet and, using a range of formatting techniques, format to enhance its appearance:

	A	B	C	D	E
1	ICT CLASS ATTENDANCE				
2					
3	Subject	Week 1	Week 2	Week 3	Total
4	Word Processing	28	25	26	
5	Spreadsheets	25	26	24	
6	Databases	22	20	18	
7	Presentations	24	25	23	
8	Communications	18	20	21	
9	Multi-media	26	26	25	
10	Average				
11	Maximum				
12	Minimum				
13					
14	Databases Viable?				
15					

3. Use a function to find the total attendance for the Word Processing classes from Week 1 to Week 3. Replicate this formula to find totals for each of the subjects. Use functions to find the average, maximum and minimum attendance for Week 1. Replicate to show results for Week 2 and Week 3.

4. Enter a logical function into cell B14 to find if the Database classes are still viable, based on the following arguments and conditions:

    If the total attendance for Databases (E6) is greater than or equal to 50, the result should be Run, otherwise Cancel.

5. Re-save the spreadsheet. Insert the filename into the header and your name into the footer.

6. Print only the cell range A10:D14, ensuring that row and column headings and gridlines will be displayed.

7. Show the formulas that you have created.

8. Print the entire spreadsheet showing the formulas, ensuring that it fits to one page and that the formulas are shown in full.

9. Resave the spreadsheet and close.

Graphs and Charts

Did You Know?

A legend is the key to the data, making it identifiable

NOTE: for more details and examples of charts, see the Functional Skills Activity Workbook and Revision Guide **Level 1**

A chart enables a user to see the results of spreadsheet data in a graphical format. Different types of data require different chart types. A pie chart is a suitable format for one data series, e.g. one row or one column of data.

Column charts are useful for showing data changes over a period of time or for illustrating comparisons among items. Line charts can display continuous data over time, set against a common scale, and are therefore ideal for showing trends in data at equal intervals.

A legend is the key to the data in the chart. A major unit is the interval between numbers on a value axis. The value axis can be displayed to start with a minimum number and finish with a maximum number.

Comparison charts

Selecting two sets of data will result in a comparison chart. The spreadsheet data is displayed as a comparison chart:

ICT Class Attendance			
Subject	**Week 1**	**Week 2**	**Week 3**
Word Processing	28	25	26
Spreadsheets	25	26	24

This is the data source containing two data series

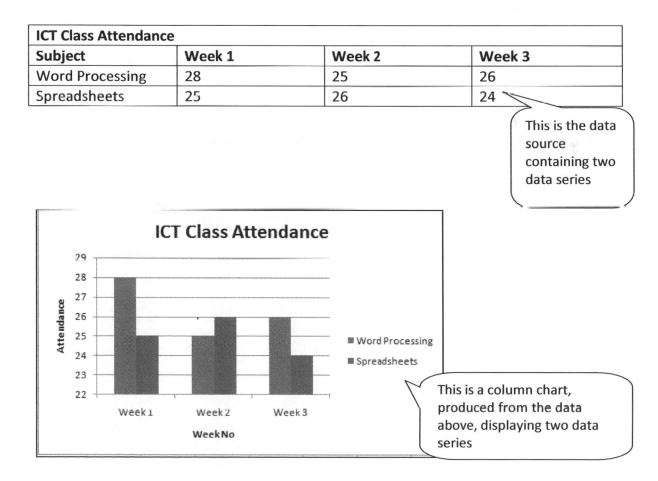

This is a column chart, produced from the data above, displaying two data series

Combined charts

A combined chart may display a column for one series and a line for another series. In the example below, the Word Processing series is displayed as a line and the Spreadsheet series is displayed as a column:

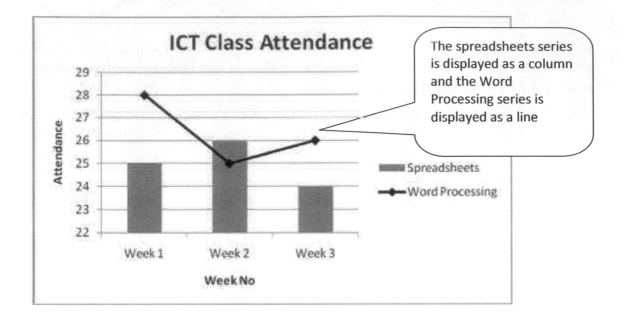

Scatter Graphs

A scatter graph, also known as an X Y chart, compares two sets of values, displayed along the vertical and the horizontal axes. See the example below:

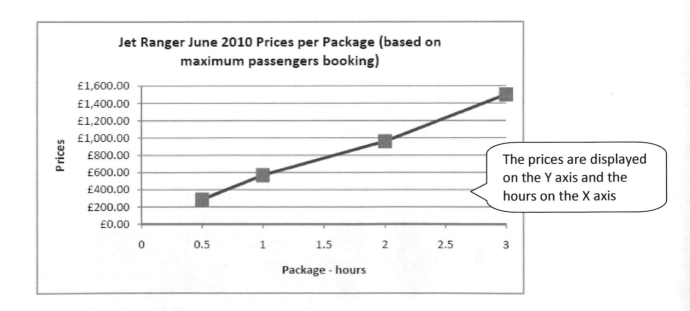

 © Lorna Bointon, Qualiteach Education 2014

To find out how to do it, follow the instructions below

Create a chart

- Select the data to be used in the chart
- Select the **Insert** tab and then, from the **Charts** group, select a chart type command

Select a chart type

Column Line Pie Bar Area Scatter Other Charts

Charts

- From the drop-down menu of the selected chart, select a sub-type.
- Move a chart to a new sheet by selecting **Chart Tools/Design** and then the **Move Chart** command. Select **New Sheet** and click OK.

Move Chart Location

Create a combined chart

- Select the data series which is to be displayed as a different chart type (to select a data series, click it once)
- Select the **Chart Tools/Design** tab and then, from the **Type** group, select **Change Chart Type**
- Choose a chart type and click OK

Change Chart Type

Apply titles

- Select the chart. From the **Chart Tools/Layout** tab and the **Labels** group, select the commands you need, such as chart title, axis titles, legend and/or data labels

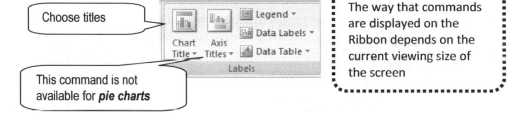

Choose titles

Chart Title ▾ Axis Titles ▾ Legend ▾ Data Labels ▾ Data Table ▾

Labels

This command is not available for *pie charts*

The way that commands are displayed on the Ribbon depends on the current viewing size of the screen

- Choose the alignment of the title(s) and enter the required text

Tip: Select **Chart Tools/Design** to change the style or type of chart and choose **Chart Tools/Format** to format the chart with different colours, gradients or textures.

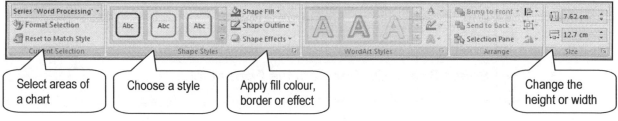

Series "Word Processing" ▾
Format Selection
Reset to Match Style

Current Selection

Abc Abc Abc

Shape Fill ▾
Shape Outline ▾
Shape Effects ▾

Shape Styles

A A A A

WordArt Styles

Bring to Front ▾
Send to Back ▾
Selection Pane

Arrange

7.62 cm
12.7 cm

Size

Select areas of a chart

Choose a style

Apply fill colour, border or effect

Change the height or width

Match Makers

Match the correct answers with the questions below:

1.	This type of chart compares pairs of values	a.	Line
2.	This type of chart compares 2 sets of data	b.	Scatter
3.	This type of chart displays 2 chart types	c.	Comparison
4.	This type of chart shows trends in data at equal intervals	d.	Combined

Enter your answers below:

1.		2.		3.		4.	

As Easy As....

A B C

1. A scatter graph is also known as.....

A	An XY chart	☐
B	A YX chart	☐
C	A line chart	☐
D	A Bubble chart	☐

2. **Finish the instruction:** To create a combined chart with columns and line, click a data series to display as the line and then....?

A	Click the **Insert** tab and then select the Line chart type	☐
B	Click the **Design** tab and then **Change Chart Type** and select a Line chart type	☐
C	Select the **Line** shape from the **Shapes** menu	☐
D	Select **Shape Outline** from the **Format** tab	☐

Practice Makes Perfect

Practical Exercise 1

1. Open the **Functions** spreadsheet that you created in the 7.1 exercise.

2. Create a comparison chart to compare the attendance for the Word Processing and Spreadsheet courses.

3. Format the chart to display a chart title and axis titles.

4. Print the chart only.

Practical Exercise 2

1. Format the chart to be a combined chart displaying the Spreadsheets series as a line chart

2. Select the Line series and format it as a different colour.

3. Format the columns as a different colour.

Practical Exercise 3

1. Create a scatter graph on a new sheet to compare the minimum and maximum attendance values.

2. Format the chart to display a chart title and axis titles.

3. Print the chart only.

4. Save and close the spreadsheet.

Databases

Did You Know?

A primary key is applied to ensure that each record is unique.

NOTE: for basic background knowledge of databases, see the Functional Skills Activity Workbook and Revision Guide **Level 1**

Field names

It is important that field headings are separated logically in order to query the data (for example, to find all customers with the surname Smith or to find customers from a specific city). A field name can be up to 64 characters long, including spaces. Microsoft® Office Access disallows the same field name within a table (duplicates). Field sizes and formats can be applied to fields. For example, a date may be formatted as a short date (01/01/2010) or a text field may be limited to 15 characters.

Example:

Incorrect
Name
Lorna Bointon

Correct	
First Name	Last Name
Lorna	Bointon

Data types

In order to organise data correctly, fields need to have data types applied according to the type of data that will be entered into the field. For example, dates should be formatted with the data type **Date/Time.** Other field data types include *Text* which is the default data type for text and alphanumeric data (e.g. data containing both text and numbers and also telephone numbers which include spaces), *Number* for numerical data with or without decimal places and *Currency* (£) for numerical data relating to costs. Data types can be selected for a field item from the Data Type drop-down list in Design View. If an incorrect data type is applied to a field in the design stage, the data may not sort properly at a later date (e.g. numerical data with a Text data type will not sort in numerical order).

Text	Allows text and numbers with a length of 255 characters
Number	Allows numbers only. Can be formatted with different settings
Date/Time	Will only allow dates or times. Can be formatted with different formats
Currency	Allows only numeric data. Format with currency symbol
AutoNumber	A numeric data type used to create a sequential record numbering system
Yes/No	This is a logical field that will enable true/false values to be entered

Primary Key

A primary key uniquely identifies a field. To set a primary key, the table needs to contain a field or set of fields that uniquely identifies each record, for example a product code or ID number. Setting a primary key allows you to link a table with another table in a database.

Primary Key

Import Text

Importing enables the user to import external data into a database from a text file without creating a link to the source file. A text file may contain data that is separated by tabs (delimited) or by commas (referred to as a csv or comma separated values file).

Validation Rule

A Validation Rule restricts data entry in a table and displays a message when unauthorised data is added (data that does not adhere to the Rule) informing the user that data integrity has been affected. For example, a validation rule can be applied to a numeric field so that only prices between specified amounts can be entered:

Validation Rule: >=30000 and <=50000
Validation Text: Only prices between £30,000 and £50,000 are allowed

Validation rules can use logical and comparison operators and be based on text, dates or numeric values. See some more examples below:

>09/09/2010   (only dates after the specified date can be entered)
<>09/09/2010   (any date **except** for this date may be entered)

Chester **or** Cardiff **or** Worcester **or** Felpham (only these 4 locations can be entered)

Not Chester   (all locations **except** Chester may be entered)

Default Values

A default value ensures that a specified value appears in empty fields. For example, a number field has a default value of 0 in blank fields, but this can be changed to any other number. A Yes/No field can have a default value of Yes or No (or no default value).

Required Text

A required field is one that requires data to be entered and cannot be left empty. If a field is set as a required field and data is not entered, a message will appear and data entry in other fields will not be allowed until data is entered into the required field

Reports

A report displays data in columnar, tabular or justified layouts and allows the user to insert headers and footers, group information under a specific field and perform calculations. Reports display data in an organised and professional format.

 © Lorna Bointon, Qualiteach Education 2014

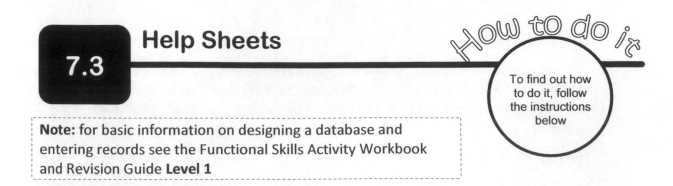

Note: for basic information on designing a database and entering records see the Functional Skills Activity Workbook and Revision Guide **Level 1**

Edit a Table

- To design the table with different field names and data types, select the **View** button and choose **Design View**.

- The table design opens enabling the user to edit the fields and field properties within the database.

Field Name	Data Type	
MEMBER ID	Number	
FIRST NAME	Text	
LAST NAME	Text	
DATE OF BIRTH	Date/Time	
MEMBERSHIP TYPE	Text	
JOIN DATE	Date/Time	
DIRECT DEBIT?	Yes/No	

A Primary key makes a field unique

Field names can be edited here

Data types are selected from here. Text is the default data type for new fields.

Field Properties

General | Lookup

Field Size	Long Integer
Format	
Decimal Places	Auto
Input Mask	
Caption	
Default Value	
Validation Rule	
Validation Text	
Required	No
Indexed	Yes (No Duplicates)
Smart Tags	
Text Align	General

Validation rules can be entered here

Field properties, default values and required values can be entered here

- Once edited, the table should be re-saved. Click the **View** arrow and choose **Datasheet View**. The **Save Table** message appears. Click **Yes**.

Insert a New Field

- To insert a new row, in Design View select a field below where the new row is to be inserted and click the **Insert Rows** button. Enter the field name and then click the Data Type arrow and choose a data type.

Delete a Field

- To delete a field, select the field and then click the **Delete Rows** button. Click **Yes** to confirm the deletion.

Validation Rules

- In Design View, select the relevant field and then press F6 to move to the Properties of that field. In the Validation Rule box enter the validation rule. In the Validation Text box enter message text that will appear if unauthorized data is entered.

Validation Rule	
Validation Text	

Required Text

- Select the field to have the required field.
- Click into the **Required** field property and click the arrow. Choose **Yes.**

Required	No
Indexed	Yes
Smart Tags	No
Text Align	General

Default Value

- Select the field to have the default value.
- Click into the **Default** field property and enter the Default value.

Primary Key

- In Design View select the field to be made unique. Select the **Primary Key** button

Reports

- Select the **Create** tab and then, from the **Reports** group, select **Report Wizard**.
- Select the table or query on which the report will be based. Next choose the available fields that will appear on the report (click a field and then click > to select individual fields or click >> to select *all* fields). Click **Next**. Skip the next step by clicking **Next**. Skip the next step by clicking **Next**.
- Choose a layout and orientation and click **Next**.
- Choose a style and click **Next**.
- Enter the report name and click **Finish**.

Import text

- From the **External Data** tab, select **Text File** (from the **Import& Link** group). Click **Browse** to find the text file.
- Select the file and click **Open**.
- Select the **Import the source data into a new table in the current database** button and click OK. Select **Delimited** and then **Next**. Ensure that the **First Row Contains Field Names** tick box is *selected*. Select **Next.** Skip the next bit by clicking **Next**. Exclude a primary key from the imported data, by selecting **No primary key.** Select **Next.**
- Enter the table name and click **Finish**. Select **Close**.

Page Layout

- Change the orientation of the table from **Portrait** to **Landscape** by selecting the **File** tab**, Print** and then **Print Preview** and then selecting the **Landscape** button.

Match Makers

Match the correct answer to the questions below:

1.	This field property restricts data entry		a.	Default value
2.	This field property ensures that data is entered in this field		b.	Primary key
3.	This field property ensures that a specified value appears in an empty field		c.	Validation rule
4.	This makes a field unique		d.	Required

Enter your answers below:

1.		2.		3.		4.	

As Easy As....

A B C

1. Which of the following formats is best suited to presenting data in a professional manner?

A	A table	☐
B	A form	☐
C	A report	☐
D	A query	☐

2. In order to edit a field, which view must be selected?

A	Print Preview	☐
B	Datasheet View	☐
C	Design View	☐
D	PivotTable View	☐

Practical Exercise 1

1.   Create a new database called **Stock.accdb** in Microsoft® Access

2.   Create a new table within the Stock database called **Products** with the following design.

3.   Keep the ID field as this will provide a unique reference for each record:

Field Heading	Data Type	Field Size/Format
Stock Item	Text	40
Quantity	Number	Integer
Price	Currency	Currency

4.   Make the Price field a Required field

5.   The Default Value for the Quantity field is 10 as this is the minimum quantity of stock allowed

6.   Create a validation rule for the Price field so that only prices over 1.99 can be entered. Ensure that a message with appropriate validation text will be displayed if the rule is violated

7.   Switch to Datasheet View, saving the table.

8.   Return to the design view of the table to edit the ID field. Rename this field as Stock ID.

9.   Add the following data to the table:

10.   Print the table, ensuring that the data can be seen clearly

Stock ID	Stock Item	Quantity	Price
1	Keyboard	100	£25.99
2	Optical Mouse	120	£6.99
3	Roller Mouse	100	£3.99
4	Mouse mats	90	£2.99
5	Memory sticks2GB	120	£12.99
6	Memory sticks 1GB	120	£12.99
7	Optical Mouse	100	£9.99

Practical Exercise 2

1.   Create a report from the **Product** data

2.   Ensure that all data can be seen clearly and add an appropriate heading for the report.

3.   Print the report

4.   Save and close the **Stock** database

Search & Sort Data

Did You Know?

Filters can be used to find data in a spreadsheet and a database

NOTE: for basic instructions on sorting on one level and using search criteria and comparison operators, refer to the Functional Skills Activity Workbook and Revision Guide **Level 1**

Sorting on more than one field

Data can be sorted in Microsoft® Access database or a Microsoft® Excel spreadsheet on more than one level:

Stock ID	Stock Item	Quantity	Price
1	Keyboard	100	£25.99
2	Optical Mouse	120	£6.99
3	Roller Mouse	100	£3.99
4	Mouse mats	90	£2.99
5	Memory sticks2GB	120	£12.99
6	Memory sticks 1GB	120	£12.99
7	Optical Mouse	100	£9.99

Unsorted data

Stock ID	Stock Item	Quantity	Price
1	Keyboard	100	£25.99
6	Memory sticks 1GB	120	£12.99
5	Memory sticks2GB	120	£12.99
4	Mouse mats	90	£2.99
2	Optical Mouse	120	£6.99
7	Optical Mouse	100	£9.99
3	Roller Mouse	100	£3.99

Data sorted on one field: **Stock Item**. The Quantity field remains unsorted

Stock ID	Stock Item	Quantity	Price
1	Keyboard	100	£25.99
6	Memory sticks 1GB	120	£12.99
5	Memory sticks2GB	120	£12.99
4	Mouse mats	90	£2.99
7	Optical Mouse	100	£9.99
2	Optical Mouse	120	£6.99
3	Roller Mouse	100	£3.99

Outermost field

innermost field

Data sorted on two fields: **Stock Item** and **Quantity**. Note how the Quantity field is now sorted after the Stock Item sort (compare the Quantity for the Optical Mouse items – the item with a quantity of a 100 now appears before the item containing a quantity of 120

Deciding on sort order

Before performing a sort on more than one field, it is important to decide which field is the *outermost* field and which is the *innermost* field (the innermost field is sorted first but will display as the second sort). In the example above, the **Stock Item** field is the *outermost* field and the **Quantity** field is the *innermost* field. To perform the sort above, the Quantity field is sorted in ascending order first, followed by sorting the Stock Item field in ascending order.

Searching

Data within a Microsoft® Access database or a Microsoft® Excel spreadsheet can be filtered on one or more fields to find specified information using *search criteria* and comparison and logical operators.

A query is a search tool in Microsoft Access Databases which also uses *criteria* to find information within a table of data.

A filter can be used in a database or a spreadsheet to filter information to find specific data. Both filters and queries use criteria, comparison operators and logical operators.

Sample data:

Product Code	Product	Quantity in stock	Price
001	Roller ball Mouse	50	4.99
002	Ergonomic keyboard	100	24.99
003	Mouse mat	200	3.99
004	Ergonomic mouse	150	43.99

Using Comparison Operators

> Greater than (e.g. entering the criterion **>150** beneath the **Quantity in Stock** heading would find the Product Code 003)

< Less than (e.g. entering the criterion **<150** beneath the **Quantity in Stock** heading would find the Product Codes 001 and 002)

>= Greater than and equal to (e.g. entering the criterion **>=150** beneath the **Quantity in Stock** heading would find the Product Codes 003 and 004)

<= Less than and equal to (e.g. entering the criterion **<=150** beneath the **Quantity in Stock** heading would find the Product Codes 001, 002 and 004)

Using Logical Operators

Logical operators are referred to as Boolean operators when used in an Internet search.

AND (e.g. entering the criteria **<4** beneath the **Price** heading and **>150** below the **Quality in stock** level on the **Criteria** row would result in one record being found for Product Code 003)

OR (e.g. entering the criteria **>4** beneath the **Price** heading on the **Criteria** row and **>150** below the **Quality in stock** level on the **OR** row would result in all of the records being found. It would find all records with a price greater than £4 *or* records with a quantity in stock of more than 150)

NOT (e.g. entering the criteria **Not >4** beneath the **Price** heading on the **Criteria** row would result in only product code 003 being found). The **<>** comparison operator can be used in the same way as NOT

Search using partial criteria

Sometimes it is necessary to search for data with only partial information at your disposal. For example, you may want to search a spreadsheet or database for an item of data that begins with a specific character or contains specific characters.

Begins with   selecting **Begins with** and entering the character **'t'** would find all items of data in the selected field/column that starts with this letter (e.g. **the, terrain, technology** etc)

Ends with   selecting **Ends with** and entering the character **'t'** would find all items of data in the selected field/column that ends with this letter (e.g. **not, greet, Clipart,** etc)

Contains   selecting **Contains** and entering characters **an** would find all items of data that contain these letters (e.g. **phantom, ant, than, aunt, advance** etc). The Does Not Contain operator will *exclude* specified characters from a search

Equals   selecting **Equals** and entering a word would find all occurrences of that word. The Does Not Equal operator will *exclude* specified words from a search

Wildcards   the **wildcard *** symbol can be used in place of characters within a word. For example, specif* will find words that begin with the letters [specif], e.g. **specify, specified, specific, specifically** etc. *een would find words that **end** with the letters [een], e.g. **green, canteen.***and* would find words that contained the letters [and], e.g. **operand, handover, band** etc. To replace only one character in the search keyword, use the ? symbol (e.g. **specifi?** will find **specific** but not specifically or specify/specified).

 © Lorna Bointon, Qualiteach Education 2014

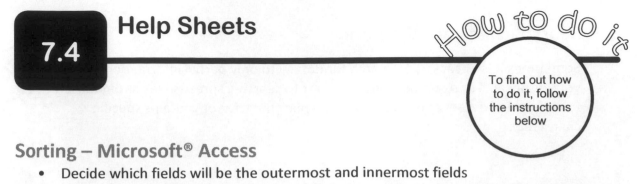
Sorting – Microsoft® Access

- Decide which fields will be the outermost and innermost fields
- Select the column/field to be sorted first (the innermost field which will appear as the second sort) and then click the required sort button from the **Home** tab and the **Sort & Filter** group.

Descending order

Ascending order

- Select the outermost column/field to be sorted (the outermost field which will appear as the first sort) and then click the required sort button from the **Home** tab and the **Sort & Filter** group.
- Click the **Save** button on the Quick Access Toolbar to save the sorted table.
- Clear a sort by selecting the **Clear All Sorts** button (beneath the sort buttons)

Queries – Microsoft® Access

- Select the **Create** tab and then select the **Query Design** button. Select the table in which you want to search for data and click **Add**. Click **Close**.

Query Design

- Double click each of the fields to display them in the **Field** row of the **Query** grid
- Enter the criteria into the **Criteria** field beneath the relevant field heading
- Select the **Show** tick box to show fields or de-select the Show box to hide fields in the query results
- To sort a query, click the **Sort** arrow beneath the appropriate field name and then select a sort order (ascending or descending)
- To see the query results, select the **Run** button

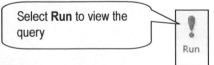

Select **Run** to view the query

Run

Simple Filters – Microsoft® Access

- Select the appropriate field and then, from the **Home** tab and the **Sort & Filter** group, select the **Filter** button

Filter

- Select the criteria and click **OK** or, if filtering numerical data, select the **Number Filters** sub-menu and if filtering text, select the **Text Filters** sub-menu. Choose a comparison operator (such as > greater than etc)

Stock ID	Stock Item	Quantity	Price	Add New Field
1	Keyboard	100	£25.99	
6	Sort A to Z		£12.99	
5	Sort Z to A		£12.99	
4	Clear filter from Stock Item		£2.99	
7				
2	Text Filters		Equals...	
3			Does Not Equal...	

☑ (Select All)
☑ (Blanks)
☑ Keyboard
☑ Memory sticks 1GB
☑ Memory sticks 2GB
☑ Mouse mats
☑ Optical Mouse
☑ Roller Mouse

Begins With...
Does Not Begin With...
Contains...
Does Not Contain...
Ends With...
Does Not En...

OK   Cancel

Select a criterion or a comparison operator

- The **Custom Filter** dialog box appears displaying the chosen filter and a box in which to enter the criteria.

Custom Filter

Amount in Stock is greater than or equal to

OK   Cancel

Advanced Filters – Microsoft® Access

- Select the appropriate field and then, from the **Home** tab and the **Sort & Filter** group, select the **Advanced** button. Select **Advanced Filter/Sort**.

- Enter the field headings into the grid.

- Enter the criteria beneath the relevant field heading.

- To apply the filter, select the **Advanced** button and then select **Apply Filter/Sort** from the menu.

- To save the filter as a query, select the **Advanced** button and then select **Save as Query** from the menu. Type in a name and click **OK**.

Advanced ▾

	Clear All Filters
	Filter By Form
	Apply Filter/Sort
	Advanced Filter/Sort...

Toggle Filter (turn on/off)

- From the **Home** tab and the **Sort & Filter** group, select the **Toggle Filter** button to switch between filtered and unfiltered data.

Toggle Filter

 © Lorna Bointon, Qualiteach Education 2014

Filters – Microsoft® Excel

- Select (highlight) the spreadsheet data. Select the **Data** tab and then, from the **Sort & Filter** group, click the **Filter** command.

- The spreadsheet data will display filter arrows in the field heading of each field. Click a filter arrow to select criteria by which to filter the information.

	A	B	C	D
1	Stock ▼	Stock Item ▼	Quant ▼	Pri ▼
2	1	Keyboard	100	25.99
3	6	Memory sticks 1GB	120	12.99
4	5	Memory sticks 2GB	120	12.99
5	4	Mouse mats	90	2.99
6	7	Optical Mouse	100	9.99
7	2	Optical Mouse	120	6.99
8	3	Roller Mouse	100	3.99

- Select a criteria or click the **Number** or **Text Filters** sub-menu to see a sub-menu displaying comparison operators:

	A	B	C	D	E
1	Stock ▼	Stock Item ▼	Quant ▼	Pri ▼	

- Sort A to Z
- Sort Z to A
- Sort by Color ▶
- Clear Filter From "Stock Item"
- Filter by Color ▶
- Text Filters ▶
  - Equals...
  - Does Not Equal...
  - Begins With...
  - Ends With...
  - Contains...
  - Does Not Contain...
  - Custom Filter...

☑ (Select All)
☑ Keyboard
☑ Memory sticks 1GB
☑ Memory sticks 2GB
☑ Mouse mats
☑ Optical Mouse
☑ Roller Mouse

[OK]   [Cancel]

- The **Custom Filter** dialog box will appear displaying the chosen filter and boxes in which to enter the criteria.

 © Lorna Bointon, Qualiteach Education 2014

> This example displays the filter Begins with. Two sets of criteria can be added using the AND or OR radio buttons

Custom AutoFilter

Show rows where:

Stock Item

| begins with ▾ | | ▾ |

◉ And ◯ Or

| ▾ | | ▾ |

Use ? to represent any single character
Use * to represent any series of characters

OK   Cancel

- Re-select the **Filter** button to switch between filtered and unfiltered data.

Show or Hide Fields

- Select the column to be hidden in the filter results and then, from the **Home** tab and the **Cells** group, select the **Format** button.

- From the **Format** menu, select **Hide & Unhide** and then select **Hide Columns**. To unhide columns, re-select the **Format** menu and select **Unhide Columns**.

Sorting – Microsoft® Excel

- To sort data in a spreadsheet table, select the data and then select the **Sort** button from the **Data** tab.
- The **Sort** dialog box opens. Select the **Sort by** arrow and choose a field heading; next select an option from the **Sort On** list arrow and then choose a sort order from the **Order** drop down list.
- Ensure that the tick box for **My data has headers** is selected.
- To sort on more than one field, click the **Add Level** button.
- The **Then by** row appears. Select a field heading for the secondary sort (innermost field) and a sort order.
- Click OK.

Sort

| ⁺ₐ⌐ Add Level | ✕ Delete Level | ▤ Copy Level | ▲ ▾ | Options... | ☑ My data has headers |

Column		Sort On		Order	
Sort by	Stock Item ▾	Values ▾		A to Z ▾	
Then by	Quantity ▾	Values ▾		Smallest to Largest ▾	

OK   Cancel

 © Lorna Bointon, Qualiteach Education 2014

Match Makers

Match the correct answer to the questions below:

1.	This can be used to replace a single character in a search word	a	*
2.	This excludes words from a search	b	?
3.	This can be used to replace more than one character in a search	c.	AND, OR
4.	These are Logical operators	d.	<>

Enter your answers below:

1.		2.		3.		4.	

As Easy As....

A B C

1. The primary sort field (sorted first in the sort results) is based on which field?

A	The innermost field	☐
B	The outermost field	☐
C	The field which is sorted first	☐
D	The primary field	☐

2. The **?** wildcard symbol does which of the following?

A	Excludes characters from a search	☐
B	Replaces one or more characters in a search word	☐
C	Represents a single missing character in a search word	☐
D	Represents a missing comparison operator	☐

130 © Lorna Bointon, Qualiteach Education 2014

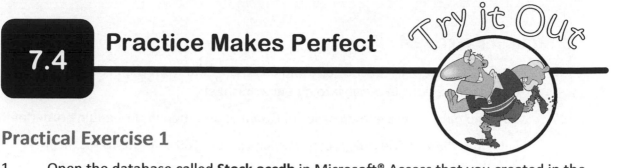

Practical Exercise 1

1. Open the database called **Stock.accdb** in Microsoft® Access that you created in the previous exercise and open the **Product** table

2. Sort the table on the following two fields: **Stock Item** (outermost field) and **Quantity** (innermost field).

Stock ID	Stock Item	Quantity	Price
1	Keyboard	100	£25.99
2	Optical Mouse	120	£6.99
3	Roller Mouse	100	£3.99
4	Mouse mats	90	£2.99
5	Memory sticks2GB	120	£12.99
6	Memory sticks 1GB	120	£12.99
7	Optical Mouse	100	£9.99

Practical Exercise 2

1. Using a query, search for stock items that match the following criteria (you will need to use a wildcard):

    Memory Sticks OR Optical Mouse AND with Price NOT less than £9.00

2. Only show the **Stock Item** and **Quantity** fields

3. Sort the query in ascending order of Quantity

4. Save the query with a suitable name and close

Practical Exercise 3

1. Use a filter to search for stock items that begin with 'M'

2. Print the filtered data

3. Remove the filter

4. Filter the data to find prices between £5 and £15

5. Print the filter

6. Remove the filter from the table

7. Close the table and exit Access.

Practical Exercise 4

1.	Open Microsoft® Excel and copy and paste the data from the **Products** database table from the previous exercise into a new worksheet

2.	Sort the data in descending order of Quantity and then in descending order of Price

3.	Filter the data to find only records which contain 100 or more items in stock (Quantity)

4.	Remove the filter and create a new filter to find Stock IDs between 2 and 5

5.	Remove the filter and create a new filter to find stock items that contains the character 'm' but does not contain 'a'

6.	Save and close the spreadsheet

Section 8 ▶

Developing, Presenting and Communicating
Information

Mail

Use communications software to meet the requirements of a complex task

Use E-mail

Did You Know?

Webmail enables a user to access their inbox from any computer

NOTE: for more information on using email, see the Functional Skills Activity Workbook and Revision Guide **Level 1**

How does email work?

An email is a means of communication via electronic mail which can be sent and received via a computer with an Internet connection, a phone line and a modem.

An Internet Service Provider (ISP) provides connectivity for a fee.

Email addresses are entered into the **To:** field and separated by a semicolon (;). The email addresses of other recipients who will receive a copy of the message should be added to the **Cc** (carbon or complimentary copy) field. An example of an email address is **contact@qualiteach.co.uk**. The first part of an email address is the *username* followed by the @ (at) symbol. The next part of the address is called the *domain name*, which sometimes includes the geographical location (UK)

Attachments

Attachments are files which are attached to an email message. For example, holiday photographs can be sent to friends as attachments in an email. A subject should be added to a message so the recipient can see what the email is about before opening it.

Be careful about opening emails and attachments from senders that you do not know. They may contain viruses or other threats that can be downloaded onto your computer or spread to other users via email.

Confidentiality

To ensure the confidentiality of an email address, enter it in the **BCC** field (blind carbon copy) and the address will be hidden from other recipients of the same email message.

Contacts

Email addresses can be stored as contacts. Having a list of stored contacts makes it easier to find and add email addresses to a message. An email address which has been added to a contact list can be displayed with a specified name, such as nickname. Other information relevant to the contact can be added, such as company, telephone number and address. A list of stored contacts is called a distribution list. Using a distribution list makes it quicker and easier to send messages to multiple recipients.

Set priority

The importance of an email message can be indicated by marking it as High Importance or Low Importance.

!

Email Signatures

Instead of typing your name, position and company name and address and telephone number at the end of an email message, you can create an email signature that contains all of these details and which will appear on every outgoing message.

Organise Messages

Outlook 2010 enables a user to organise messages by creating folders within the Inbox for storage.

Messages can be moved or copied into folders and sorted by specified types, such as by attachments.

Collaborative Tools

Collaborative tools enable users to share files, store files and work to a shared timetable online using collaborative tools such as Outlook calendars to synchronise timescales and Google Apps or Microsoft SharePoint Server for file sharing.

Appropriate Language

Use appropriate language with different recipients. For example, the tone and language style used to chat with a friend will be different to the tone and language used in a business email. Be careful about using bad language in an email as this can result in users being banned from email forums and chat rooms.

Using bad or inflammatory language is called **flaming**.

Online Communication

Other types of communication include *blogs* (web blogs) which are online diaries, *wikis* which can be edited directly from a user's browser and online forums and chat rooms which allow users to chat and keep in contact in 'real time'.

To find out how to do it, follow the instructions below

NOTE: for basic training instructions on using email, such as reading, replying and forwarding, see the Functional Skills Activity Workbook and Revision Guide **Level 1**

Outlook 2010

Create and Send an E-mail to a Contact

- To create a new email message, select the **New E-mail** button. Select the **To** field. The **Select Names** dialog box opens. Select the contact and click the **To** button. Repeat to add other contacts or lists to the **CC** or **BCC** fields. Click OK. Enter a subject and the message text and then click **Send.**

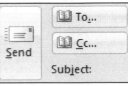

Attach a file to an E-mail message

- From the message tab, select **Attach File** from the **Include** group. Find and select the file to be attached and then click the **Insert** button. If the message is in HTML or Plain Text format, the attachments will appear in the **Attach** Field; if the message is formatted as Rich Text Format, the attachments will display in the body of the message.
- To reduce the file of a file attachment, it should be compressed into a zipped folder first.

See Chapter 2 for information on file compression

Open and Save Attachments

- Open the message containing the attached file. Double click a file attachment to open it or right click and select **Open**. To save an attachment, open the message, right click the attached file and select **Save As**. Alternatively, select **File** and then select **Save Attachments**. Select the correct drive/folder in which to save the file and click **Save.**

Priority

- Select the **High Importance** or **Low Importance** button from the **Message** tab and **Tags** group

❗ High Importance

⬇ Low Importance

Contacts

Create a Contact:

- Open an email message and right click the sender's email address. Select **Add to Outlook Contacts** and enter further details if needed, then click **Save and Close**. Alternatively, select the **Home** tab and then click **New Items** and then **Contact**. Enter details for the contact and click **Save and Close**.

Create a Contact/Distribution List:

- Select **Home ▸ New Items ▸ More Items ▸ Contact Group.** Type in a name for the list. Click the **Add Members** button. Choose **From Outlook Contacts.** Select the contacts that you want to include in the distribution list and then click the **Members** button. Repeat to add all contacts to the list. Click **OK.** Click **Save and Close.**

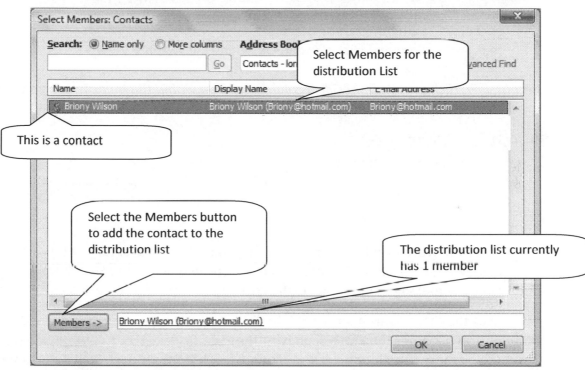

Edit or Delete a Contact:

- *Edit:* select **Contacts** from the navigation pane. A list of all your contacts will be displayed in the right hand pane. Double click a contact to make changes to the existing details and then click **Save and Close**.
- *Delete:* select **Contacts** from the navigation pane. A list of all your contacts will be displayed in the right hand pane. Right click a contact and then select **Delete** from the shortcut menu (alternatively select **Delete** from the **Home** tab/**New** group).

Add a Contacts List to an Email Message:

- Open a new message and select the **To** field. The **Select Names** dialog box opens. Select the distribution list 🔳 and click the **To** button. Repeat to add other contacts or lists to the **CC** or **BCC** fields. Click OK. Enter a subject and the message text and then click **Send.**

Organise Messages

Sort Messages

- Select **View** tab, click **Change View** arrow and then click **Manage** V**iews**
- Ensure that **<Current View Settings>** is selected. Select **Modify**
- Select the **Sort** button - the current sorting order is indicated on the right hand side of the button.
- The **Sort** dialog box will appear, click the **Sort items by** list button and select a field. Ensure that the correct sort order radio button is selected (e.g. **Ascending**) and click OK then OK again. Click **Apply View**

Alternatively, click the arrow beside a column heading within the Inbox to sort in ascending (upward arrow ▲) or descending (downward arrow ▼) order.

Search for Messages

- Click into the Search box:

- Enter the word into the **Search** box. As you type the word, relevant messages containing the search characters will be displayed below the Search box.
- Only the message(s) that meets the criteria that you entered will be displayed
- Click the **Close Search** button [x] to display all messages (the magnifying glass Search button becomes the Close Search button).
- To see more search options, e.g. **From** (search from sender), **Sent To** (search for recipient), **Subject** (subject text), click into the Search box to see the Search Tools Ribbon. Select a command from the Search Tools ribbon and then enter the search criteria in the search box.

- To use the Advanced Find feature, select the **Search Tools** arrow and then select **Advanced Find.**
- Enter the search word(s) and choose the location of the search words (e.g. subject field and message, subject field only etc), the address of the sender, the address of the recipient and then select **Find Now.**

To close the Search Tools tab, select the **Close Search** button.

 © Lorna Bointon, Qualiteach Education 2014

Folders

- To create a new folder, click the **Inbox** icon in the **Navigation pane (Folder pane)** and then select **Folder ▸ New Folder.**
- The **Create New Folder** dialog box will appear
- From this box you can select the appropriate location for the new folder.
- Select **Inbox** (if not already selected) and then enter the **Folder Name** and click OK.
- The new folder will appear in the Navigation pane alongside any existing folders within the **Inbox** folder.

Move Messages into a Folder

- Select the message and then select **Home ▸ Move.**
- Select a folder from the drop down menu or select **Other Folder.**
- The **Move Items** dialog box will appear.
- Select the appropriate folder from within the **Inbox** and click OK.
- Open the **Inbox** folder (click the + beside the folder or double-click to view the contents of the **Inbox** folder).
- Open the new folder to view the contents. The moved message is now in the new folder but not displayed within the **Inbox** folder.

To copy messages, repeat the above procedure but use the **Copy to Folder** command

Delete and Restore Messages

- Select a message and then click the **Delete** button. Confirm the deletion.
- Deleted messages will be sent to the **Trash** folder. To restore a recently deleted message to your inbox, first open the **Trash** folder, select **Home ▸ Move** and then select **Other Folder.** Select the **Inbox.** Click OK. The message will have returned to the inbox.

Empty Deleted Items

- To permanently empty the contents of the **Trash** folder, right click the folder and select **Empty Folder.** Click **Yes** when the delete confirmation message appears

Create an email signature

- Open a new message
- On the **Message** tab, select the **Signature** arrow and then **Signatures**
- Select **New** and then enter a name for the signature and click OK
- Enter name and other details to appear in the signature. Format as required
- Select the **New Messages:** arrow and choose the signature name. Repeat to add the signature to replies and forwarded messages
- Click OK

 © Lorna Bointon, Qualiteach Education 2014

Outlook Calendar

- Select **Home** ▸ **New Items** ▸ **Appointment**
- Enter the Subject:
- Enter the Location:
- Set the Start Time and the End Time
- To ensure that you receive a reminder, click the **Reminder** arrow and select a time option from the drop down list (you can also set a sound for the reminder by clicking the **Sound** option at the bottom of the menu).
- Check or uncheck the All day event tick box as required.
- If the meeting will be repeated, set up a recurrence by clicking the **Recurrence** button on the toolbar.
- Set a day/time. Click OK
- Select the **Save and Close** button
- Click on Calendar in the navigation pane. Select how you want to view the calendar (by Day, Week, Month)
- To edit the appointment double click the calendar entry
- The **Open recurring item** dialog box will appear. Select **Open the series** and click OK.

Outlook To-Do Lists

- Select **Home** ▸ **New Items** ▸ **Task**
- Enter a subject for the task
- Select a Due Date and the Start Date
- Select In Progress as the status.
- Set the priority as required
- Set the % complete as required
- Ensure that the Reminder tick box is checked and set a reminder for a specified time
- Enter a note if required and click **Save & Close.**
- If you haven't completed the task by the specified time a reminder will be issued. You then have the option of dismissing the reminder, opening the item or clicking Snooze so that you get reminded again in 5 minutes time (or other time that you set). If you have finished the task you can select Open item and set the Status to Complete. The course timetable task would then appear scored through in the Task pane

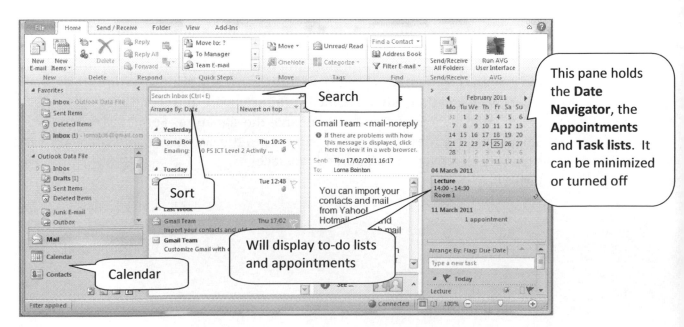

Match Makers

Match the correct answer to the questions below:

1.	Google Apps is an example of a ...	a.	Distribution list
2.	Received messages can be organised by creating	b.	Collaborative tool
3.	A list of contacts is called a	c.	Synchronise timescales
4.	Outlook calendars can be used to....	d.	Inbox Folders

Enter your answers below:

1.		2.		3.		4.	

As Easy As....

1. This allows access to email from any computer, anywhere in the world?

A	Outlook Express	☐
B	Webmail	☐
C	Podcast	☐
D	wiki	☐

2. Why should you be careful about opening an email from an unknown sender?

A	It may contain marketing information	☐
B	It may contain a virus	☐
C	It may be meant for some else	☐
D	There is no need to be careful	☐

Practical Exercise 1

1. Create a new email message with the subject **Organise** and send it to yourself.

2. Create a folder called **Manage** in the Inbox

3. Move the **Organise** message into the **Manage** folder

Practical Exercise 2

1. Create a new message with the subject **Functional Skills.**

2. Attach a file that you have created from one of the previous exercises to the **Functional Skills** message and send it using your own email address

3. Open the Functional Skills message and save the attached file to a drive on your computer.

Practical Exercise 3

1. Create a contacts list called **Colleagues** with the following addresses and information:

    Jane Warden |jw@qualiteach.co.uk | Supervisor | ICT Department | ext 304

    Brian Jones | bj@qualiteach.co.uk| Manager | Engineering Department |ext 305

    Hardeep Kapoor |hk@qualiteach.co.uk| Line Manager |Printing Department | ext 306

2. Create a new message and add the Colleagues contact list to the **To** field. Enter your own email address in the Bcc field.

3. Send the email.

4. Amend the Contacts list so that Jane Warden's email address is **jw@qualiteach.co.uk**

Practical Exercise 4

1. Using the Outlook Calendar, set an alarm for next Monday at 9:am

2. Add an entry for the first Tuesday of next month for a staff meeting at 1:00pm in the Executive Room

Stay Safe and Respect Others

Did You Know?

Personal information posted online can be used in identity fraud

Confidentiality

To ensure the confidentiality of an email address, enter it in the **BCC** field (blind carbon copy) and the address will be hidden from other recipients of the same email message.

Before sending a message or photographs to recipients in a contacts list, think about whether it is appropriate to send it to each of the recipients in the contact list. Some of the recipients may not know each other and may not want others to see their photos or email address or other details. Ask permission before sending photographs of people to other recipients.

Respect Others

Always use appropriate language when communicating on a social networking group or chat room/forum. Be careful not to use inflammatory or bad language or be insulting or disrespectful to others. Using bad language or language designed to make people angry is called **flaming** and can get a user banned from online forums. Be careful to respect the views of other people and be tolerant towards gender, age or cultural differences. Always ask permission before communicating another person's views or opinions.

Stay Safe

It has become increasingly important to take care of personal details since the advent of social networking sites (a social networking site is a site, such as Twitter or Facebook, where a user posts details about themselves and allows other people to communicate with them via instant messaging and email).

Users of social networking sites should be careful about what information they post about themselves and others. Always ask permission before posting any information or photos of other people. To prevent identity theft and fraudulent use of your personal details, it is good practice to limit the people who can view your personal details to specific friends and family members. To avoid the possibility of a stranger using your details for fraudulent purposes, you should never provide the following information on a social networking site:

- Your address
- Your date of birth
- Photographs containing you or friends
- Telephone number
- Email address

Online Security
Passwords

Never give your password to anyone else. A bank will never ask you to give them your password, so do not reply to requests via email for your personal details or password. This is likely to be a scam called *phishing* which is used in identity theft (see below).

A password should be changed regularly and kept secret. It is important that you use a strong password. This means using random letters, symbols and numbers that cannot be easily guessed.

An example of a strong password: **TnJKL18$*@**

A weak password is one that can be easily guessed or 'cracked' by a fraudster. Examples of weak passwords are:

- Mother's maiden name
- Your date of birth
- Your birthplace
- Your name
- The word 'password'
- Using the top line on the keyboard (e.g. QWERTY or 123456)

SPAM

This is the name given to unsolicited mail, usually received from companies trying to sell something or from fraudsters who get personal details by deceiving users into clicking a web link within a message and then providing details, such as personal details, e.g. name, address, date of birth, and security details, e.g. username and password. Some virus programs also send out SPAM mail. Never reply to unsolicited mail or you will end up on an active SPAM list and will continue to receive bulk mail. Do not click any web links or adverts within an email message from an unknown recipient. Some Spammers use 'web 'beacons' designed to send a message back to the sender once the message is opened. Therefore, it is safer to delete suspect messages without opening.

Webmail usually has its own Spam filters installed which send suspect email messages to a folder before being deleted at a specified time (once a week, month etc). For users of email client software, such as Outlook, spam filtering software can be installed to identify and prevent unwanted messages.

Phishing and Identity Theft

Phishing is the term used to describe the process of fraudulently gaining personal information through devious online methods. For example, a user may receive a message supposedly from their mobile phone company, asking them to click a click within the message to go to the company's website and log in and provide other personal information.

This information can then be used in identity theft. A reputable company will never ask for your log in details, so delete any messages that request these details.

Spyware

Spyware is software that secretly monitors a user's online activity by tracking key clicks and other online activity. Anti-spyware software should be installed to prevent identify and threats whilst online. Adware refers to a program that displays advertising on a user's computer, usually in the form of 'pop-ups'. Adware advertising is designed to target the user and based on results from spyware monitoring of a user's web browsing habits

Firewalls

A *firewall* should be installed to prevent unauthorised access to a computer system (called *hacking)*. A firewall can also be used to block a user's IP address, therefore preventing them from being identified online.

Online Hoaxes

An online hoax may come in many guises, such as a scam message that appears requesting the user to click a link to gain a prize; pop up ads or messages that inform the user that a virus or threat has been detected and requesting that the user clicks a button or link to scan the computer; chain mail that uses implied threats and bad luck warnings to make the user forward the message to other recipients; chain mail may also offer get rich schemes.

Always check the email address carefully in messages; scam mail often disguises itself with an email address *similar* to an email address from a reputable company, but with some small differences. Be suspicious of any messages that claim to be *urgent!!!* or which offer money.

Match Makers

Match the correct answers to the questions below:

1.	A firewall should be installed to prevent this	a	SPAM
2.	This is the name given to unsolicited mail	b	Phishing
3.	These may claim to be urgent or offer money	c	Hacking
4.	The term used to describe fraudulently gaining personal information through devious online methods	d	Hoaxes

Enter your answers below:

1.		2.		3.		4.	

As Easy As....

1. You receive a message supposedly from your bank asking you for your log in details. What should you do?

A	Click the link as requested but do not enter your details	☐
B	Reply to the message asking them to stop sending you SPAM mail	☐
C	Delete the message	☐
D	Click the link and enter your details	☐

2. Which of the following is considered a strong password?

A	Date of birth	☐
B	Pet's name	☐
C	Mother's maiden name	☐
D	A random mix of letters and numbers	☐

Section 9 ▸

Developing, Presenting and Communicating Information

View

Combine and present information in ways that are fit for purpose and audience

Combine and Present

Did You Know?

It is important to maintain data integrity when combining information

Integrating Information

Information can be combined for a variety of purposes, such as:

- A presentation combining text, pictures, charts and spreadsheets
- A webpage containing text, video, animations, audio and images
- A folded leaflet containing text, images, charts
- A newsletter containing text, images, charts and tables

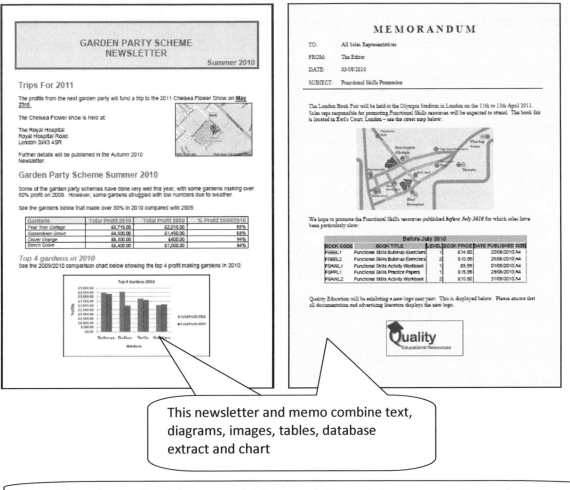

This newsletter and memo combine text, diagrams, images, tables, database extract and chart

Leaflet with text, drawing, map, spreadsheet extract and chart arranged in 3 columns

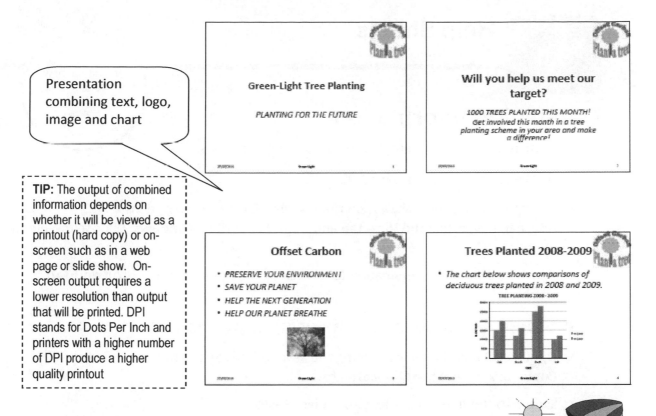

Presentation combining text, logo, image and chart

TIP: The output of combined information depends on whether it will be viewed as a printout (hard copy) or on-screen such as in a web page or slide show. On-screen output requires a lower resolution than output that will be printed. DPI stands for Dots Per Inch and printers with a higher number of DPI produce a higher quality printout

Fit for Purpose

Fit for purpose and audience means that the combined information is suitable for the intended viewer or reader (audience). Commercial media producers, such as newspapers and magazines, research their audience thoroughly to ensure that the product is fit for purpose, e.g. meets the needs and expectations of a set of people, and to determine average age group, interests and gender of the intended audience.

Ensuring that the product meets the needs of this reader means making the content snappy!

House style

House style refers to the layout, style and formatting of documents. House style includes layout and styles (such as fonts, sizes, alignment, indents and tabs). It is good practice to use a consistent house style to enhance appearance and give a professional look to documents.

The house style of this letter includes letter head with logo, margins, line spacing, fonts and sizes and alignment

How to do it

To find out how
to do it, follow
the instructions
below

Combining Information

For help on inserting images and tables, see previous sections.

Switch between open windows

- Open files will display as tabs on the task bar. Click a tab to open the file. Alternatively, select the **View** tab and then click **Switch Windows**. Choose the file to open.

- **Tip:** A shortcut key combination for switching between windows is **Alt** and **Tab**.

Insert graphs/spreadsheet data using copy and paste

- Open Excel and the file containing the graph/chart. Select the graph and click the **Copy** button from the **Clipboard** group.

- Switch to the open document and select **Paste**.

Insert movies and sounds in MS PowerPoint

Movie clips:
- Select the **Insert** tab and then, from the **Media** group, click **Video**.

- Select **Video from File**.

- Locate the video file and click **OK**.

- Videos can also be inserted from the Clip Art Video gallery. Select this option from the Video menu, and then choose a movie/video clip from the task pane.
- The Video Tools/Format and Playback tabs become available when the video clip is selected. Select Playback to choose how it will start (on click or automatically)

Sound files

- Select the **Insert** tab and then, from the **Media** group, click **Audio**.

- Select **Audio from File** if it is saved on your computer, or select from **Clip Art Audio** option to insert a sound from the Clipart gallery.

- Locate the sound file and click **OK**.
- The Audio Tools/Format and Playback tabs become available when the audio clip is selected. Select Playback to choose how it will start (on click or automatically)

Checking Techniques

Did You Know?

Proofreading means checking each word thoroughly

NOTE: this section contains crossover material from Level 1

Proofreading

It is important to ensure that a finished publication or document is free from errors. Mistakes appear unprofessional and can detract from the intended message being conveyed within the document.

Proofreading means checking every word carefully to ensure that text is accurate and that meaning is clear. Proofreading also covers layout and presentation of a document and ensures that the language style is appropriate. Proofreading literary work is performed by book editors/publishers and proofreading agencies.

Check layout and style

The layout of a document should be appropriate for the information or message it is trying to convey and should be suited to the correct age group, gender or specific interest of the reader. For example, a poster for a party will use a different layout and style to a formal business letter.

Check for meaning

The meaning of information within a document or publication should be clear and free from bias or prejudice. It is important that text and images are checked to ensure that the meaning is being conveyed correctly.

Spell Check

Each of the Microsoft® Office applications contains a spelling tool which will check text for accuracy. When a spelling error is found, it is displayed in the Spelling dialog box with suggestions for correct spellings. Be careful about relying entirely on the Spelling tool and proofread text carefully. The Spell Check facility will display words that are not in its dictionary, as errors, such as proper nouns, e.g. first and last names and scientific words. Some spelling errors may not be identified if the spelling matches another word – for example, typing 'to' instead of 'too' (**to** is a correct word but if used in the wrong context instead of **too** it will not be identified as a spelling error – for example, *'It was to much'*).

Preview

To ensure that the layout and page structure is correct and appropriate for the type of information it contains, the document or publication should be previewed before printing. Previewing work before printing ensures that paper wastage is kept to a minimum and ensures professional output.

To find out how to do it, follow the instructions below

Check Spelling

- **Microsoft® Word, Excel and PowerPoint**: From the **Review** tab and the **Proofing** group, select the **Spelling & Grammar** command (Word) or the **Spelling** command (Excel, PowerPoint)

  ABC ✓ Spelling & Grammar

- **Microsoft® Access**: From the **Home** tab and the **Proofing** group, select the **Spelling** command

  ABC Spelling

- The Spelling tool will display spelling errors and provide suggested replacements. Select a suggestion or click **Ignore** if you know that the word is correct (click **Ignore All** to ignore all instances of the word or **Change All** to change each instance of the word to the suggested spelling). A dialog box will appear at completion of the spelling check. Click OK to confirm.

The error will be displayed here

Suggested spellings are displayed here

Ensure that the correct language is displayed

Spelling and Grammar: English (U.K.)

Not in Dictionary:

Thiss informationn iss presented in ssingle linne spacing and is left aligned.

Suggestions:

This
This's
Thiess

☑ Check grammar

Options...   Undo

Ignore Once
Ignore All
Add to Dictionary

Change
Change All
AutoCorrect

Close

Click **Ignore Once** or **Ignore All** to move on without correction if you know the word is correct

Click **Change** or **Change All** change the word to the suggested spelling

Undo the last correction if you make a mistake

Match Makers

Match the correct answers to the questions below:

1.	For a document to meet the needs of the intended audience it must be...	a.	House style
2.	Conforming to this ensure consistency in business documentation	b.	Proof reading
3.	This should be higher for printed output	c.	Fit for purpose
4.	This involves checking each word carefully	d.	Resolution

Enter your answers below:

1.		2.		3.		4.	

As Easy As....

A B C

1. Which of the following documents can be combined with charts and tables?

A	A sales report	☐
B	A newsletter	☐
C	An information sheet	☐
D	Any of the above	☐

2. An error has been made in the following text: **the cat sat _in_ the mat.** Which of the following statements is correct?

A	The error will be identified by the Spelling command	☐
B	The error will be identified by the Grammar checking facility	☐
C	The error will be identified by proofreading	☐
D	The error will not be identified by any of the above methods	☐

Practical Exercise 1

1. Create a new document and enter the following text including the deliberate spelling errors:

> The kat satt in the mat. The rane on Spain falls mainly on thee plain.

2. Use a combination of proof reading and spell checking to check and correct the text that you have just entered.

3. Save the document as **check.docx** and close

Practical Exercise 2

1. Open the newsletter about your hobbies that you created in a previous exercise (Ex 6.1a).

2. Create a pie chart that shows the popularity of your hobbies as percentage values

3. Paste the chart into your newsletter, ensuring that it fits between the margins and is shown in full

4. Insert the shape that you created in Exercise 6.1c into the newsletter

5. Ensure that the chart and shape and any other content is arranged appropriately.

Section 10 ▶

Developing, Presenting and Communicating Information

Judge

Evaluate the selection, use and effectiveness of ICT tools and facilities used to present information

Evaluation Techniques

Did You Know?

Evaluation should take into account strengths and weaknesses

NOTE: This section contains some crossover material from Level 1

What is Evaluation?

Evaluation means reviewing the usefulness of ICT tools that have been used to complete a task.

This may require considering whether other ICT tools could have completed the task more quickly or easily. Evaluation should be completed at each stage of a task and also at the task's completion to ensure that ICT tools will effectively achieve the desired result.

Factors to consider:

There are many ICT tools which can be used to create, develop and present information in a variety of different formats. It is important to think about how the information will be displayed e.g. as printed output or viewed on screen.

Strengths and Weaknesses

An important part of the evaluation process is consideration of the strengths and weaknesses of the ICT tools used to complete a task. A strength may be that the chosen ICT tool can process information faster or automate certain tasks, making them quicker to perform and increasing accuracy. A weakness may be that the ICT tool was harder to learn and use and training may be required (this affects the time and cost of a task).

Costs and Benefits

These are important parts of the evaluation procedure. How costly are the chosen ICT tools? Costs can be measured in terms of cost and time. The cost of purchasing software to perform a task or the amount of time invested in learning how to use the software can be measured against the result. If the task was quicker and easier to perform and the results are more professional and improve overall productivity, then the benefits may be considered to outweigh the costs.

Other considerations are:

- **Duration** – how long has it taken to complete the task using the chosen ICT tools. Could the task be completed using less time and money with different ICT tools?
- Different **file formats** - consider whether some files may need to be saved in a different file format or software version so that other users can access them.
- **Results** – could you have achieved better results using different software packages and tools?
- **Downloading** – think about length of time taken to download large file sizes. Could smaller file sizes be achieved by saving files in other file formats? Consider the speed of an internet connection and whether this could be an issue when downloading files from a web page.

- **Fit for purpose** – is the finished product suitable for the intended audience and has feedback been provided?
- Are any improvements necessary?

An evaluation sheet should contain the following:

- Type of task e.g. presentation
- The ICT tools used to complete the task e.g. Microsoft® PowerPoint
- Actions taken to ensure that the result is fit for purpose, e.g. proofreading, checking layout, format and accuracy
- A consideration of what worked and what didn't work so well, e.g. did the digital (sound/video) content make the presentation more exciting or more distracting?

Example:

Evaluation of ICT Tools

Task Name: Create a slide show

ICT Tools used Microsoft PowerPoint

Could other ICT tools have done the job better? No

Actions taken to ensure that work is fit for purpose:

The slide show used a master slide to ensure consistency and animations to create interest. The slide show contained information that will interest sales reps working for the company and used charts to show numerical data

What went well and what didn't go so well?

Too many animations distracted from the content. Using audience handouts allowed the audience to make notes.

Match Makers

Match the correct answers to the questions below:

1.	Improved productivity is considered to be a?	a.	Fit for Purpose
2.	Decreased productivity is considered to be a?	b.	Strength
3.	This means it is suitable for the intended audience?	c.	Time
4.	Costs can be measured in money and this?	d.	Weakness

Enter your answers below:

1.		2.		3.		4.	

As Easy As....

A B C

1. Why is it important that a task is evaluated at each stage in the task and at completion?

A	So that changes and improvements can be made at each stage and at completion	☐
B	So that changes and improvements can be made at the end	☐
C	So that it remains the same without changes throughout the stages	☐
D	It isn't important as a task only needs to be evaluated at completion	☐

2. Which of the following actions could be taken to make a product 'fit for purpose'?

A	Proofreading	☐
B	Check spelling	☐
C	Check layout and format	☐
D	All of the above	☐

Answers ▶

Mark

Answers to Matchmakers and Easy As questions

1.1 Activities

Match Makers

1.	B	2.	D	3.	A	4.	C

1e, 2c, 3d, 4a, 5b

As Easy As

1a

2a

2b – A storyboard is used to make a rough design, enabling placement of text and images, and to create a navigation structure

3d

4a

2.1 Activities

Match Makers

1.	E	2.	C	3.	A	4.	G	5.	F	6.	B	7.	D

As Easy As

1C, 2C, 3B, 4B

2.2 Activities

Match Makers

1.	C	2.	D	3.	A	4.	B

As Easy As

1A

2.3 Activities

Match Makers

1.	D	2.	C	3.	A	4.	B

As Easy As

1D

2.4 Activities

Match Makers

1.	C	2.	D	3.	B	4.	A

As Easy As

1D

2.5 Activities

Match Makers

1.	D	2.	A	3.	B	4.	C

As Easy As

1B

3.1 Activities

Match Makers

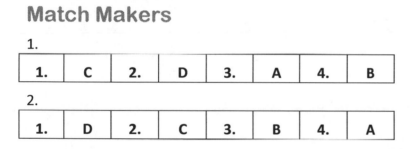

1.

1.	C	2.	D	3.	A	4.	B

2.

1.	D	2.	C	3.	B	4.	A

As Easy As

1D, 2A, 3A, 4C

4.1 Activities

Match Makers

1.	B	2.	D	3.	A	4.	C

As Easy As

1B

5.1 Activities

Match Makers

1.	C	2.	A	3.	D	4.	B

As Easy As

1D, 2D

6.1a Activities

Match Makers

1.	D	2.	B	3.	A	4.	C

As Easy As

1D, 2D

6.1b Activities

Match Makers

1.	D	2.	A	3.	B	4.	C

As Easy As

1B, 2D

6.1c Activities

Match Makers

1.	C	2.	D	3.	A	4.	B

As Easy As

1C, 2D

6.1d Activities

Match Makers

1.	C	2.	A	3.	D	4.	B

As Easy As

1C, 2A

7.1 Activities

Match Makers

1.	B	2.	C	3.	D	4.	A

As Easy As

1B, 2C

7.2 Activities

Match Makers

1.	B	2.	C	3.	D	4.	A

As Easy As

1A, 2B

7.3 Activities

Match Makers

1.	C	2.	D	3.	A	4.	B

As Easy As

1C, 2C

7.4 Activities

Match Makers

1.	B	2.	D	3.	A	4.	C

As Easy As

1B, 2C

 © Lorna Bointon, Qualiteach Education 2014

8.1 Activities

Match Makers

1.	B	2.	D	3.	A	4.	C

As Easy As

1B, 2B

8.2 Activities

Match Makers

1.	C	2.	A	3.	D	4.	B

As Easy As

1C, 2D

9.1&2 Activities

Match Makers

1.	C	2.	A	3.	D	4.	B

As Easy As

1D, 2C

10.1 Activities

Match Makers

1.	B	2.	D	3.	A	4.	C

As Easy As

1A, 2D

 © Lorna Bointon, Qualiteach Education 2014

THE MANCHESTER COLLEGE
COLLEGE LIBRARIES
ASHTON OLD ROAD
MANCHESTER
M11 2WH

Lightning Source UK Ltd.
Milton Keynes UK
UKOC01f1027150614

233360UK00003B/31/P

9 780956 573148